W9-BMN-202

SLIPCOVER
CHIC

SLIPCOVER CHIC

Illustrations by Michelle Ball
Text by Catherine Revland and Carol Cooper Garey

HEARST BOOKS

NEW YORK

Copyright © 1992 by
s m a l l w o o d   a n d   s t e w a r t   i n c .

All rights reserved. No part of this book may be reproduced or utilized in any form
or by any means, electronic or mechanical, including photocopying, recording, or by
any information storage or retrieval system, without permission in writing from
the Publisher. Inquiries should be addressed to Permissions Department,
William Morrow and Company, Inc.,
1350 Avenue of the Americas, New York, N.Y. 10019.

It is the policy of William Morrow and Company, Inc., and its imprints and affiliates,
recognizing the importance of preserving what has been written, to print the books
we publish on acid-free paper, and we exert our best efforts to that end.

Library of Congress Cataloging-in-Publication Data

Ball, Michelle.
Slipcover Chic : designing and sewing elegant slipcovers at home / illustrations by
Michelle Ball ; text by Catherine Revland and Carol Cooper Garey.
p. cm.
ISBN 0-688-11433-4
1. Slipcovers.   I. Revland, Catherine.   II. Garey, Carol Cooper.   III. Title.
TT198.B26 1992
646.2'1—dc20
92-6733   CIP

Printed in Singapore
First U.S. Edition
1 2 3 4 5 6 7 8 9 10

Produced by Smallwood and Stewart Inc.
New York City

Edited by Rachel Carley
Designed by Michelle Wiener

contents

introduction 6

CHAPTER ONE

slipcover style 8

CHAPTER TWO

all about fabric 52

CHAPTER THREE

getting started 62

CHAPTER FOUR

pillow covers 88

CHAPTER FIVE

sewing a slipcover 100

CHAPTER SIX

terms and techniques A to Z 120

index 143

introduction

Slipcovers are to furniture what clothes are to people. They change with the seasons, fit tightly or loosely, and cover a variety of shapes. Much as clothes do, they follow distinct fashions. Slipcovers not only make it possible to protect good furniture, but also to give a worn-out chair or sofa a stylish new look—with far more flexibility and less cost than upholstery. And the ability to transform one piece of furniture is the beginning of changing an entire room.

Given the practicality and good looks of slip-covers, it should not be surprising that the idea of these quick-change cover-ups dates at least as far back as the Middle Ages. In that period, a single furnishing often served more than one purpose, and would be moved around a house as need be. An ordinary wooden bench, for example, might appear with an embroidered cover when placed in a room dressed for a special occasion. By the 18th century, the rich tapestry chair coverings fashionable in well-to-do households often consisted of two parts that fit separately over the backs and seats. Fastened with hooks and eyes at the corners, the covers could be easily removed and stored.

Slipcovers are mentioned in historical references in the context of both protecting fine upholstery and providing a change of wardrobe from season to season. In France and England, for example, loose covers made of linen were favored for the summer months. One well-known English portrait dating from about 1775 shows a country gentleman posed in a wood-frame dining chair whose seat and back wear a loosely fitted, one-piece cover of checked linen. That design, essentially a box shape that falls to just below the seat and leaves most of the chair legs exposed, is the ancestor of the streamlined slipcover considered stylish today.

With the evolution of decorating styles have come different views of how the slipcover should fit. One school of traditionalists insists on a form fitting and wrinkle-free look, much like that of upholstery. The other subscribes to the English country house style, which runs from semi-fitted to downright baggy. The classic American slipcover is a happy compromise: not too tight, not too loose.

While the fit may vary according to taste, the advantages of slipcovers is a subject on which most decorators concur. In fact, professionals often advise clients to have a set of slipcovers made in tandem with new upholstery so the furniture has a change of wardrobe. The investment pays off in the long-term protection of good upholstered pieces.

Some decorators favor slipcovers over upholstery because they are affordable, practical, and easy to clean. Removable covers also provide infinite possibilities for changing the look of your furnishings and the room around them. A slipcover might be gathered or flounced for a romantic look, or dressed up with silk braid, fringe, or Turkish tassels for an opulent effect. Another attribute of a good slipcover is its easy comfort; it conveys a message that says, "Come relax, and sit a while."

Perhaps the real pleasure—and surprise—of slipcovers, however, is that you don't need a professional designer's help to decorate with them. Indeed, as this book illustrates, stylish slipcovers can be created at home. Here, in one volume, is all the information needed to sew a beautiful cover, whether you are starting small with a throw pillow or transforming an expansive three-seat sofa. Included are original slipcover designs for all manner of furnishings, as well as practical tips on choosing and buying fabric, estimating yardage, and measuring and pinning patterns. Finally, there are step-by-step directions for covering pillows, ottomans, chairs, love seats, chaises, daybeds, and sofas. In short, everything you need to discover the sheer delight of decorating with slipcovers.

slipcover style

a portfolio of
imaginative design ideas

Slipping on a new cover provides countless ways to make virtually any piece of furniture—be it a sofa, love seat, chair, chaise, daybed, or ottoman—more seasonal, more durable, and more stylish. Style itself is surprisingly easy to achieve. It's really just a matter of paying attention to detail, and respecting your own personal taste. This ensures a slipcover that will be pleasing for years to come as well as one that is like no other.

Meant to spark the imagination, the designs on the following pages are offered as inspiration. Let your imagination run free, then turn to the subsequent chapters to learn how to translate your own ideas into reality.

sofas and love seats

For a summer look, a wicker sofa can wear a ticking-stripe cover, tied at the arms with matching bows. A lace hem enhances the nostalgic feeling

Perhaps the most enduring design legacy left by the legendary decorator Billy Baldwin is the slipcover. Recognizing and promoting the value of removable furniture covers, Baldwin actually recommended one set for summer and a second for winter—his own fabric preference being pale blue denim for the former and paisley cotton for the latter. The choice of inexpensive yet sturdy material made such duplicate sets an affordable and practical option.

Given how much wear a typical sofa endures, a slipcover might almost be considered mandatory. And because a sofa plays a dominant role in a room's decor, its covering is also important in establishing a keynote for other furnishings. The decorating goal, then, is to blend the piece with its surroundings,

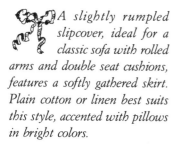*A slightly rumpled slipcover, ideal for a classic sofa with rolled arms and double seat cushions, features a softly gathered skirt. Plain cotton or linen best suits this style, accented with pillows in bright colors.*

Gathering fabric at the arms will soften the lines of a tailored sofa. A plain fabric for the back and seats can be paired with a complementary print for the skirt, whereas an overall pattern might be too much.

making sure that the sum of its pattern, color and shape harmonizes with accompanying chairs, as well as with the curtains and carpet in a room.

If the existing decor is already satisfying, the sofa cover should simply complement it, not only in the fabric choice, but also in such details as the skirt treatment and finishing trims. A slipcover, however, can also be the starting point for a new look. Virtually any type of sofa—from the small-scale, two-person love seat to the expansive sectional—adapts remarkably easily to a change of clothing, and the particular profile, style and overall proportions of a piece can be used to inspire the design of the new cover.

A traditional piece with rolled arms and fat, overstuffed cushions, for example, is likely to call for a looser, more casual fit—even a deliberately rumpled look—than is a sleek contemporary sofa. As a rule of thumb, the tighter the slipcover, the more it will imitate formal upholstery.

11

A solid-color fabric will make a diminutive love seat appear roomier and is an effective background for any type of pillow. Cotton would create a smooth effect, while a corduroy or velveteen would provide texture. Contrasting welting works well to define the graceful shapes of the classic highback sofa profile.

A floral chintz slipcover evokes an English country look. The lines of the sofa seem to disappear into a bed of flowers—providing excellent camouflage for a piece with less-than-perfect proportions. Throw pillows can be covered in a mixture of solid, striped, and floral-printed fabric.

Vertical stripes help to emphasize height, especially if lined up on both the body and skirt of a slipcover. A centered back pleat, finished off with perky bows, hides a zipper, while adding an eye-catching detail. Bows could be made from contrasting ribbon, or from ties stitched from the same fabric as the slipcover.

Contributing to a neat, almost formal appearance, a skirt of fringe is ideal for a square-edged sofa in need of some decorative interest, and saves on the extra yardage that would be required for a fabric skirt. A selection of pillows includes throws in contrasting plaids along with a jaunty striped bolster.

A slipcover in blue and white stripes calls to mind the cool, crisp texture of shirting and creates a refreshing look for a change of seasons. Fabric sleeves draped over the arms and tied with self-welting offer an unexpected flourish. The box cushions are fitted into two-piece seat covers for a comfortable overstuffed look.

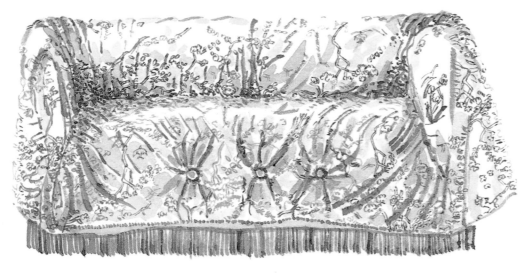

If large enough, a vintage drapery panel can become an instant slipcover. Extra fabric is loosely tucked behind the seat cushion, while existing button pleats appear custom-made.

A chevron print becomes a striking cover for a high-back sofa with a well-defined profile. A directional pattern such as this cannot be railroaded, but must run vertically over a piece. The extra-short skirt strikes a lighthearted mood, while a pile of pillows helps de-emphasize the large, flat back.

The loose cover associated with "casual chic" works best on a rounded sofa with plump cushions. Paisley pillows with flanged hems highlight the seat cushion.

15

A sectional sofa can gain new life from a change of cushion covers. Fabric should be chosen carefully when dealing with such a large expanse, since big pieces tend to control a decor. To tone down the fabric, throw pillows could be dressed in complementary solids.

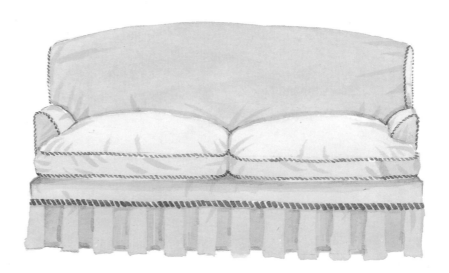

A slipcover in a pale color is the ideal backdrop for cording that picks up the same color in a darker shade.

Soft green velvet dresses a channel-back love seat (right) with simple elegance; each channel can be welted for added definition.

With its unobtrusive profile, a traditional three-seat sofa with rounded arms takes on the delicate character of its fabric. Care should be given to the placement of dominant motifs when a fabric has a striking overall pattern. Here, the flower clusters are lined up on the skirt.

one sofa
three looks

Slipcovering a sofa is easiest when starting with a piece that has "good bones," like this classic two-seater with a strong frame, pleasing proportions, and ageless curves.

Such a basic shape will never go out of style. Yet, as the three designs here show, it can easily adopt another personality, depending on the slipcover it wears. Assuming a formal identity, the handsome piece might be dressed in striped satin with a skirt tucked into sharp box pleats. In a floral print, it looks ready for a garden room, while plain cotton and contrasting welting suggest a feeling of cool simplicity.

Wide stripes dignify the two-seater and accentuate its shapely back. Such stripes also have an enlarging effect, making a sofa seem grander. When folded into box pleats, they appear as a solid fabric.

In this version, a host of plump pillows covered in the same floral print enhances the garden-like quality of the design. A ruffled skirt creates a much softer profile than box pleats.

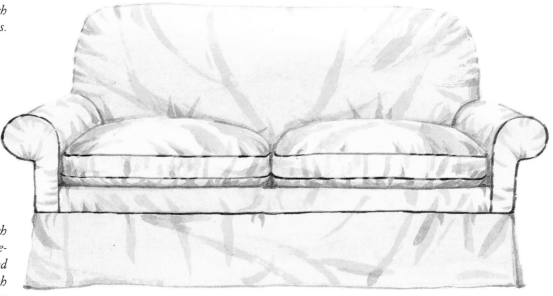

A no-frills approach to slipcovering results in understated sophistication. Accented with welting, this easy-fitting cover with a tailored skirt derives its effect from clean lines.

chaises and daybeds

Function has always dictated the appearance of furniture. As body-length seats, for example, chaises and daybeds were originally fashioned for relaxation, and their look is synonymous with comfort. The classic chaise, in fact, is really nothing more than an extended arm chair with a built-in ottoman. Clothed in a pretty cover with a floor-length skirt, such a furnishing is especially at home in the private confines of a bedroom, offering an inviting place to curl up with a book.

Consisting of an oblong cushion set on a frame, a daybed, on the other hand, works well as a sofa, tossed high with pillows for comfort. When the pillows are removed, this versatile piece is ready for a night's sleep.

Although luxury fabrics are also appropriate, the traditional chaise, complete with down-stuffed cushion, will endure additional years of wear if it is slipcovered in heavy cotton or linen. A seat-to-floor flounced skirt adds a note of luxury.

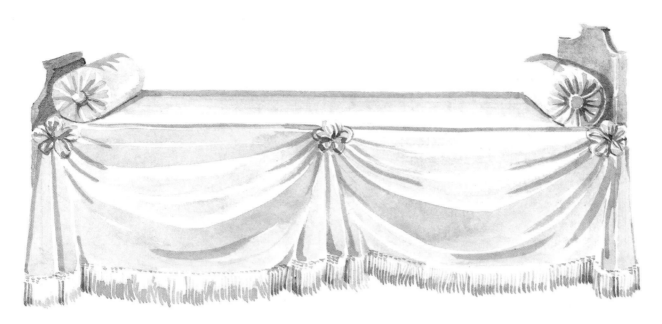

Draped over a day-bed cushion, a ready-made bedspread becomes an instant slipcover when caught into swags. The rippling gathers are echoed on the bolsters.

A wood-framed day-bed acquires interest from plump throw pillows covered in bright prints that bring color into the scheme. The overall effect conveys a feeling of informal comfort.

A contoured foam daybed lends itself to a casual throw. This inventive quick–change slipcover requires no sewing.

A one-arm chaise offers an easy fit for a slipcover. An airy pattern with a white background can make a piece look bigger.

Folded in half, one futon becomes an instant daybed; two can be stacked for extra comfort. Durable canvas or broadcloth works well for this style.

A skirt tucked into crisp box pleats distinguishes a simple daybed. Tasseled bolsters, used as "arms," and pillows in striking prints are strong accents.

one daybed
three looks

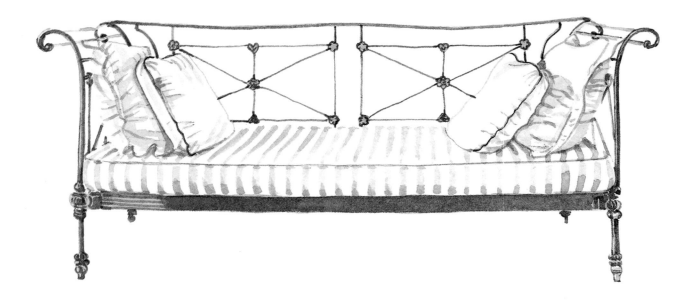

Whether the frame is plain or elaborate, the essential form of a daybed is simplicity itself: one long cushion and a few pillows for a back rest. The same piece can look entirely different depending on how the cushion is covered, and how much of the frame is concealed or left exposed. Here, an antique iron piece illustrates an evolution in slipcover style—from spare, to tailored, to elegantly romantic.

In the simplest version, striped cotton ticking covers the oblong cushion, letting the iron frame stand on its own. Using just a few cushions keeps the look understated.

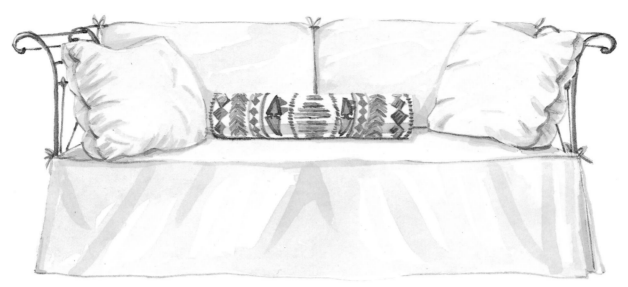

Draped right over the seat cushion, a paneled skirt is knotted to the ironwork with self-ties. Here, back cushions and throw pillows obscure the frame.

As glamorous as an evening dress, a richly trimmed slipcover completely transforms the iron daybed. Overlaid with a fringed swag, a gathered skirt is draped under the seat cushion.

chairs

Developing in response to evolving cultural customs—and to the manner in which people choose to sit—the chair has probably undergone more stylistic changes through time than any other type of furnishing. Until the Middle Ages, for example, a chair was a rather extravagant possession, reserved for honored family members or guests. With its straight back and square seat, it held the sitter erect and dignified.

By the 18th century, furniture had changed, designed to reflect comfort as well as rank. Chair

Two variations of the armchair are closely related by slipcovers made from the same fabric. Simple lines and a tailored skirt give the straight-back chair a tidy appearance, while a looser fitting cover with a long, scalloped skirt suits the curved-back design. Wide stripes focus attention on the flared arms of both styles.

Tied Grecian style, three layers of sheer, softly pleated gauze make a graceful cover for a slipper chair. The fabric is draped on one layer at a time and tucked in to fit the chair back as the tasseled cord is crossed and knotted. Slipstitching secures the trim to the chair top; otherwise, no sewing is required.

backs grew slanted and straight lines gave way to curves. This relaxation of posture eventually produced the easy chair, with its thick, upholstered seat and rounded arms.

Now chairs are available for every occasion and room style. In the category of the easy chair, for instance, there is the all-upholstered design with arms. This can take the form of a high-backed piece with wings for warding off drafts, or a low-slung club chair, often used in pairs as an accompaniment to a sofa. Still another classic known for both ease and versatility is the upholstered slipper chair. With its dainty appearance, this low-seated armless style is likely to be found in a bedroom or dressing room.

Not surprisingly, the wide variety of chair designs suggests a corresponding diversity in slipcover styles. A new cover can emphasize the existing shape of a chair, or, conversely, diminish unappealing features. A slipcover with a full skirt, for example, will do a thorough job of concealing unsightly legs. On the other hand, a side chair with a handsome frame that deserves to be seen might be partially slipcovered, perhaps just on the seat.

The fit of a slipcover also contributes to the overall style. Loose covers create comfortable-looking chairs, as if they were wearing slightly oversized robes. Form-fitting styles, by contrast, follow a chair's profile and minimize wrinkles. The two types of fit can also be combined, as when a short, loose jacket is layered over a snug, longer underlining.

Such a dual treatment also opens up opportunities for mixing fabrics. Indeed, many designs are enriched when different fabrics are used in tandem and layered for texture and shape. The result is a slipcover that not only derives dimension from the chair, but provides it as well.

A distinctive back cover permits the ornate legs of a straight-back side chair to stand out. The glove-like cover, secured with self tabs at the bottom, is stitched from a plain cotton hand-painted with a floral medallion. A similar effect may also be achieved with embroidery on the front, back, or both.

An all-over print lends a delicate air to a round-backed side chair. The gathered skirt gains extra flair from an underlayer in contrasting stripes, while the deliberately short cover shows off the chair's fluted legs—just as a skirt would a pretty ankle.

An ordinary seat cover becomes something more when contrasting fabrics are paired. For extra character, the skirt is neatly box-pleated following the repeat of the plaid pattern. Stripes running in opposite directions would also be effective. Oversized buttons secure the cover at the back corners.

A variation on the seat cover is the simple box style, fashioned with side pieces and a back flap. Such detailing is a good idea for dining chairs that are stationed at the table, and thus only seen from the back.

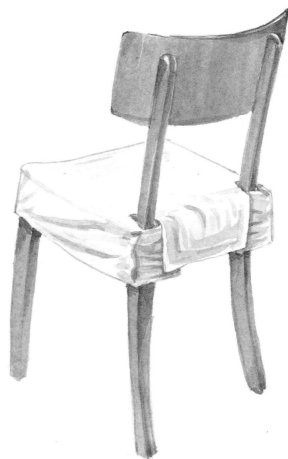

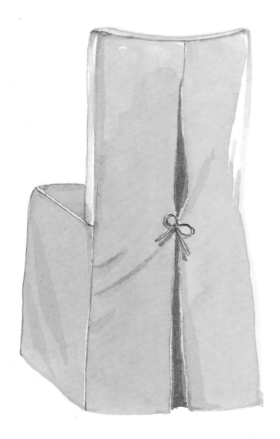

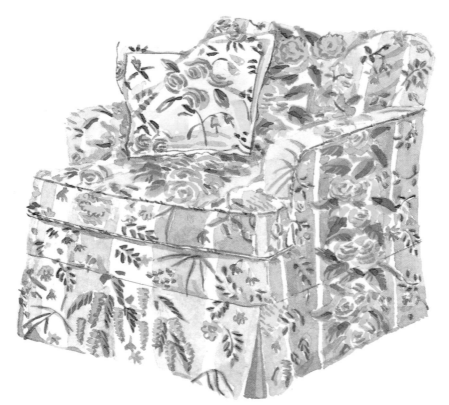

A single bow is all the decoration needed for a basic cover. A crisp cotton in a solid color is a good choice for this classic slipcover style stressing clean lines and a vertical profile. The back pleat is ornamented with contrasting lining.

A lively chintz can rejuvenate almost any armchair, including the low-backed club chair. The cabbage-rose pattern is carefully lined up on the back and sides. Such traditional treatments as the tailored skirt and self-welting are appropriate finishes for this familiar chair style.

Contrasting solids distinguish an unusual double slip-cover designed for a director's chair. In blue, the bottom layer consists of a box cover for the chair. Next, simple panels are stitched together and laid on top like a tunic. Knotting the panel ends adds extra flair.

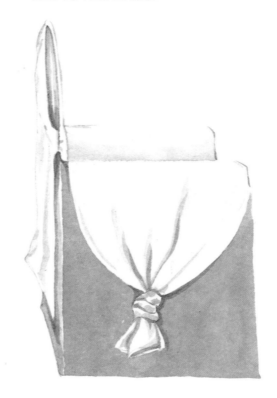

A delicately proportioned chair lends itself to a slipcover in a small print that inspires interest without being overwhelming. Designed as a sheath, the cover hugs the round back and squared arms, falling in pleated panels to the floor.

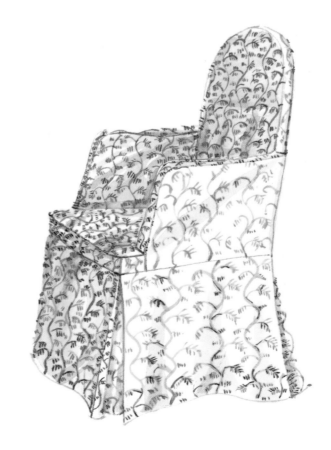

Although it wouldn't hold up for another type of slipcover, a sheer fabric such as organdy will stylishly dress a dining chair. This slipcover recalls the transparent draperies traditionally used to cover furniture during hot summer months in the American South.

A period chair becomes young in spirit when novel covers are slipped over both the back and seat. Tied on with bows, the covers are trimmed with gold metal star buttons that also appear on the skirt.

Floral-sprayed chintz is a natural for a refreshing slipper chair cover. A scalloped skirt, an alternative to the more conventional straight hem, gives the design a sprightly character.

A small-scale slipper chair is suited to a romantic slipcover style with deep flounces and a pretty back bow. The lively plaid fabric could be changed to chintz for a summer look or even taffeta for the Christmas season.

The loose slipcover associated with English country houses is appropriate for a roomy round-back armchair. Casual tucks ease the fabric around the curve of the back, while welted seams create a tidy finish for the skirtless cover. A fabric pattern with a distinctive repeat would also be effective on the long back.

A piece of fabric draped over the seat and arms of a chair, then tied around the back, makes an easy yet original slipcover. A large shawl or a fabric panel with the edges hemmed works well, but the piece must be long enough to permit a good knot.

Checks look just right on a traditional arm chair and are ideal for a summer style. This cover is enhanced with jaunty rickrack edging and a side pocket designed to hold reading material.

A distinctive double-layered slipcover derives character from a shirred underskirt overlaid with tassel-tipped panels. The top of the cover consists of a solid-colored fabric that points to the generously curved profile of the back and arms; the throw pillow is covered in the same fabric as the underskirt.

A bold stripe lends stature to a sizable wing chair with handsome cabriole legs. This form-fitting style makes the most of the chair's strong lines while self-welting finishes the cover with a neat, trim look.

A softly draped slip-cover brings elegance to a classic club chair. With a skirt gently pleated to the floor, the cover follows the curves of the piece—but not too tightly. The look is comfortable and easy. A ruffled throw pillow picks up the colors in the slipcover fabric.

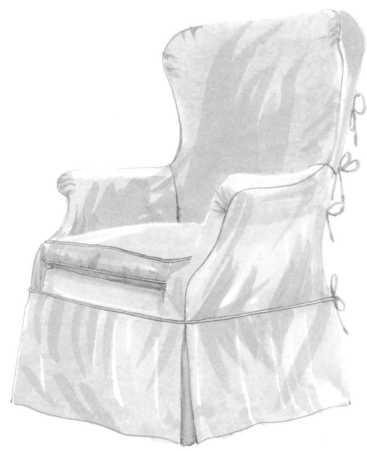

An apron-like cover, with bow ties fastening front to back, encases a traditional wing chair with style while eliminating the need for a zipper. Self-welting trims all the edges and the paneled skirt. The flowing lines and solid color accentuate the cover's striking simplicity.

A mix of plain and patterned fabric brings interest to an arm—chair slipcover. The print fabric, used for the inverted pleat, also appears on the cover of the seat cushion.

See-through organdy transforms a low-seated slipper chair (below). The flared skirt is gathered gracefully at each corner of the seat, then falls straight to the floor. A wide border helps the skirt hold its shape.

Grosgrain ribbon trim highlights the tight fit of a slipcover that hugs the frame and seat of an overstuffed bedroom chair (far right). The skirt flares slightly, adding pleasing fullness.

one chair four looks

Splashed with an attractive pattern of hydrangeas and roses, a floral-print slipcover creates the fresh look of a spring garden. The fabric says it all. No trim other than self-welting is needed.

An upholstered armless slipper chair, with a separate seat cushion and curved back, can be used equally effectively as an accent piece in the bedroom, dressing room, or living room, or grouped with several others around a table for comfortable dining.

This familiar chair style, shown here in four different sets of dress, takes well to a straightforward slipcover with a neat fit, requiring little, if any, ornamentation. What most changes the look of the chair is the style of the skirt, which can be tailored with tight box pleats, flared for a pretty profile, or gathered into soft, full flounces.

The broad, flat surfaces of the back and seat make this chair ideal for large, overall floral prints or bold stripes. Solid colors, on the other hand, yield a subdued impression. Sewing two covers would make the most of the chair's functional design, as this simple seating piece can be moved easily from room to room.

As crisp-looking as a summer awning, this modest tailored slipcover is adaptable to any decor. The skirt border provides body, emphasizing the box shape.

A handsome cover for the armless chair is fashioned with solid-colored cotton canvas tied at the back with bows. The panelled skirt has pleated corners for elegant simplicity.

Toile de Jouy, a scenic fabric often associated with romantic bedrooms, turns the chair into a charming accent piece. A flared skirt makes a small piece seem larger.

ottomans

 *Gathers caught with a knotted sash form a stylish cover for a low, round ottoman.*

A scalloped hem adds flair to a square-sided ottoman cover. An unsual hem or border will stand out even more when layered over a dark underskirt.

Probably the most adaptable piece of furniture ever invented, the ottoman is also among the most mobile, and can thus suit almost any occasion or use. One day it might be a footstool or an extra seat by the fire, the next a convenient place to set down a breakfast tray.

Because they are subject to a fair amount of wear and tear, ottomans are natural candidates for slipcovers, which might be used to camouflage worn-out upholstery, or just as a fresh change of clothing for any piece, new or old. And since ottomans are generally small and compact, with basic rectangular or circular forms, they readily lend themselves to a broad range of slipcover styles.

The simplest cover of all might be nothing more than a pretty scarf draped over the existing upholstery and perhaps caught with a length of cording. Conventional skirted treatments, in gathers or box pleats, serve well, but there is also plenty of room for taking creative liberties.

Try topping a small bench with a patterned cushion, for instance, or stacking three cushions for an uncomplicated, yet effective design. A bit of heavy fringe or braiding can also dramatically change the character of an ordinary cover.

40

A covering of pale green silk endows a round ottoman with formal elegance. Shown off to advantage by the rich fabric, heavy fringe and matching cording pick up the green while adding new color accents.

A compact stacked ottoman design consists of three separate cushions, each slipcovered in matching fabric. Self-welting cut on the bias creates crisp edges. Cushions covered in three different fabrics would create a whimsical look.

A pleated ottoman cover features corner lacing crisscrossed through grommets and an underskirt in another color. For this style, coordinated prints can be just as effective as contrasting solids.

A rectangular ottoman takes on a pleasing softness when a shirred cover is slipped over the base. This, combined with the tightly fitting case for the top cushion, creates the look of upholstery.

A loose cover gathered softly at the corners provides a relaxed look for a rectangular ottoman. The cording is tied on to hold the gathers in place. Backed with a different fabric, this slipcover can be reversible.

An ad-hoc ottoman can be improvised from a bench topped with a slipcovered bed pillow. Green-and-white awning stripes are an especially good choice for a summer feeling.

The simplest of round covers in a jazzy animal print transforms a four-legged stool. Several of these covers can be on hand for variety or a quick change.

A free-flowing floral pattern accents the romance established by a fully gathered skirt. This traditional slipcover style is adaptable to all manner of prints and solids.

The tailored skirt with corner kick-pleats is a slipcover classic, particularly suitable to cottons that will hold the inverted folds. This unpretentious style is easily matched to other furnishings in a room.

one ottoman
six looks

The most basic ottoman—the round, four-legged foot stool—offers infinite opportunities for creative slipcovering. This one conventional type can take on strikingly different looks, depending on the fabric patterns, the trims, and the style of skirt, which can be gathered, tailored with corner kick pleats, or folded into a series of box pleats.

Any of these covers can work for a footstool meant to accompany a chair, but they are also distinctive enough to help an ottoman stand on its own as an original accent piece. Even flea-market finds are easily rejuvenated with these covers. As long as the frame holds its shape, the condition of the upholstery doesn't matter.

Box pleats give this style a neat, tailored appearance. The cushion is stitched with matching welting for a smooth fit.

A loosely flowing cover can slide on over textured upholstery. Easy to stitch, this style features a skirt that falls from a simple circular top.

In a gypsy-inspired style, contrasting fabrics are layered. The top piece is simply a cotton scarf; the corners can be knotted, or trimmed with hefty tassels. Under the paisley-print square, a circle of cotton is designed as a fringed "petticoat."

When stitched in a plain cotton or linen, a classic skirted cover can be a backdrop for eye-catching trims. Here, buttons and bows are a clever touch.

Stitched on after the cover is completed, twisted cording and grosgrain ribbon are an attractive alternative to self-welting.

Luxurious trims and a textured fabric such as velvet will effect a dramatic appearance. Covering half of the ottoman, overlapping fringes create the illusion of more height.

45

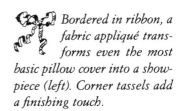

An elegantly shirred round pillow (left) features a floral medallion centered on the front. Twisted cord conceals the single seam line.

A simple bolster (below) is an ideal addition to a daybed. This classic oblong pillow lends itself to a form-fitting cover.

pillows

Pillows are among the most useful and versatile elements in home decor, and even just a few bring added comfort and color to a room. They can be equally effective as single accents or tossed into colorful piles.

Depending on their size and and shape, these adaptable accent pieces might become seat cushions, throws, or boudoir pillows. Oblong bolsters are

Bordered in ribbon, a fabric appliqué transforms even the most basic pillow cover into a showpiece (left). Corner tassels add a finishing touch.

A ruffled round (below) becomes soft and feminine with a cover stitched from a pretty floral fabric. This traditional style adapts equally well to prints and solids.

especially great additions to a daybed, in effect becoming its "arms." Whatever their use, all pillows derive their character not only from the fabric that covers them, but also from such trimmings as tassels, ruffles, and appliqués.

Cording twisted into "frogs" at each corner finishes a boudoir pillow (right). The essence of simplicity, this classic style lends itself to an infinite range of trimmings.

An easy bolster cover (far right) can be made from a single piece of fabric, joined with one seam and pulled into gathers at each end with a drawstring.

A flange, or tailored hem, forms a crisp border for a European square (below). These oversized pillows are typically used to dress up a bed, but can be transplanted to any room.

Fabric cut on the bias lends a pleasingly comfortable shape to a throw pillow stuffed with down (right). Contrasting cording runs along the seam line.

A plump Turkish pillow (right) calls for a sturdy covering. Heavy vintage fabrics, such as damask and silk faille, will yield a rich look for the cover top. A piece of tapestry is a good alternative.

47

details

A wool rosette becomes an elegant accent when a double layer of ball fringe is added.

The decorative details used to finish a slipcover are as important to its character and individuality as the fabric itself. Used effectively, trim becomes a form of punctuation. Uplifting and surprising, tassels and fringe serve as exclamation points. Final and definite, braid and gimp mark endings in the way periods do. And buttons and bows, like hyphens, hold things together.

All of these forms of ornamentation are known as *passementerie*, decorating's grand finale. The word, from the French, evokes images of the elaborate layers of heavy trimmings that did so much to define the 18th-century Roccoco style—a look that was celebrated and revived by the Victorian taste for lavish ornament. Today, trimmings tend to be used more sparingly. Rather than overwhelming an article of furniture, they have become important complements—beautiful on their own, yet important for highlighting style and form.

In slipcovering, trimmings are the starting point for real creativity. Some can be effective details—a rosette marking the back of a slipper chair, perhaps, or a twisted cord edging the sides a cushion. Trims can also become an element of the cover itself. Thick fringe, for example, will make a handsome and unusual skirt for a sofa or ottoman. More than merely decorative, however, such finishing touches as braid, fringe, welting, ribbon, ruffles, tassels, bows, and buttons serve important functional roles, concealing seams and defining shape.

Cording is especially effective when several colors are twisted together.

Embroidered ribbon is best shown off against a solid-color fabric.

Ribbon takes on an entirely different character when woven through with slender cording.

Banded cording can be sewn on through the loops.

Bordered fringe is designed to be stitched to a seam.

One important consideration affecting trim selection is color. Edgings and tassels generally work best if they pick up a shade found in a patterned slipcover fabric. When used with a solid, they can be effective in a contrasting color that makes them stand out.

Another factor is placement. A tassel or bow, for instance, can help set off a detail such as a pleat or to mark the shoulders of a chair.

A buttoned wool tassel swings from a bolster.

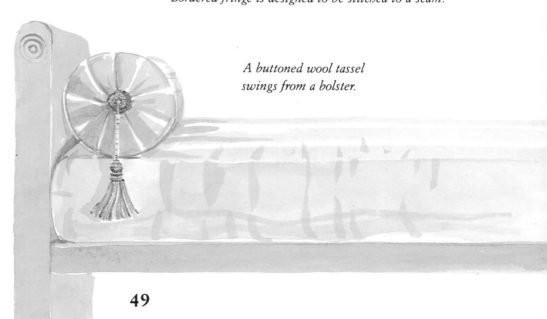

Tasseled edging can be used to trim a pillow, and makes a pretty finishing touch along a seam line.

Buttons are as useful and decorative on slipcovers as they are on clothes.

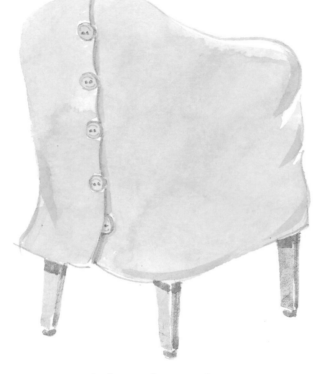

As this simple, sporty slipcover shows, the placement of trimmings doesn't have to be predictable. Here, bows or medallions would be equally effective.

A tassel can be hung from a button or a rosette for rich detail.

Tiny tassels add dimension and movement to a cheerful version of classic straight fringe.

Twisted cords of multicolored satin make up a bright trim suitable for finishing cushions. The woven edge offers a border for easy stitching.

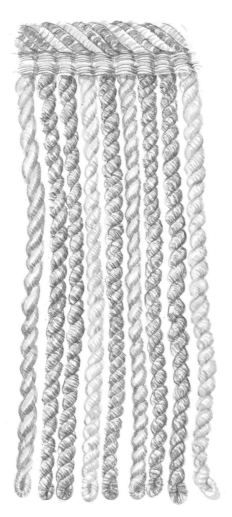

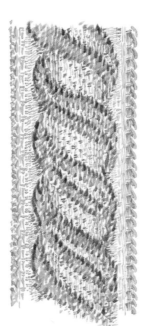

Twisted into loops, cording can provide tailored definition.

Accenting the colors of the slipcover fabric, a wide ribbon of silk brocade can be used to make a striking border.

Deep fringe makes a dramatic chair skirt. Paired with a solid-color fabric, it is bold, but not overwhelming.

A chenille button can be used alone as ornament, or stitched on to anchor a tassel.

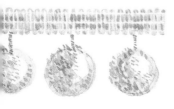

Traditional ball fringe made of clipped cotton features a woven ribbon easily stitched to any slipcover.

Glamorously long, twisted-cord fringe tends to have a move-ment all its own and is an alluring addition to a skirt hem.

all about fabric

The most critical decision in any slipcovering project is your choice of fabric. The material that dresses your furniture contributes not only to its appearance but also to its life span, and is just as important to slipcovers as it is to more permanent upholstery.

There is no question that buying good-quality yardage will pay off in many years of wear. Equally significant, however, is the decorative impact the fabric has. Pattern,

color, and weight play a role, both in the way a particular cloth relates to the shape and style of the furnishing itself, and how it fits into an overall decorating scheme.

Before making a purchase, bring home samples and drape them over the furniture to be covered. Live with them for a week or two. Experiment by mixing textures and patterns. While there are many decorating guidelines, you will find no hard and fast rules. Your choice will rest on what looks and feels right to you.

decorating with fabric

Choosing fabric generally involves an evolutionary process. If you're not sure how to begin, start looking through as many decorating magazines and books as possible. Inspiration can also be found in the decorators' show houses held periodically, usually in spring and fall, in most regions of the country.

Another idea is to compile a scrapbook, filled with photos, fabric swatches, and paint chips, as well as any available samples of what is already in your house. Serving as an overall guide in your search, this portable reference will be a great help in narrowing down the choices.

Most importantly, however, you should simply stand in the room where the slipcover will find its home, taking time to look around—not only at the sofas, love seats, and chairs that may already be there, but also at the carpet and area rugs, pillows, wallpaper, and curtains. Imagine the room with new fabric, in a different color or pattern, covering all the seating pieces. What are your goals? To effect a seasonal change, to communicate a specific mood or style? Who is the room for and how is it used? The more questions of this sort that you raise, the closer you will come to focusing on your needs and tastes, and ultimately to making a satisfying choice.

Florals on a white background will usually produce an airy, lighthearted feeling.

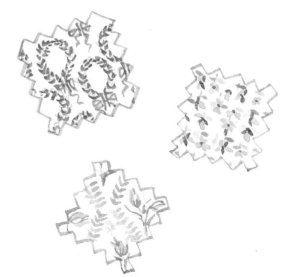

color and pattern

It is impossible to overemphasize the importance of fabric to your decor. Its color and pattern are powerful tools that can be used effectively to shape the look and feel of a room. Dark colors and subdued prints might be used for a quiet look, or pastel floral patterns for a romantic effect. Similarly, certain colors and patterns are associated with certain seasons. The quintessential summer look, for example, is achieved with whites. Cooling and expansive, whites present no conflict. They don't compete with any colors or patterns, and they are compatible with all furniture styles, from period antiques to sleek contemporary designs.

The color green evokes a summer freshness and can make a room seem cooler.

Certain shades also suggest a sense of the outdoors. No color accomplishes this evocation better than green, as the famed American decorator, Elsie de Wolfe, demonstrated as early as the 1940s. Come summer, she ritually dressed the furniture in her New York apartment in fern-printed chintz slipcovers that complemented curtains of matching

Contrasting patterns like those used on these club chairs and accompanying accent pillow can be effectively mixed when they share a color or motif that ties them together.

chintz and leaf-green walls. Due to her influence, fern prints have become summertime classics.

By contrast, paisley, another classic, is an all-season choice, favored for its rich colors and adaptability to a variety of decorating styles. The English penchant for throwing a wool paisley shawl over a chair has generated a fashionable look for winter, while paisley-printed chintz has become a fresh option for warmer months.

Another scheme that transcends the seasons is black-and-white, the possibilities for varying texture and pattern being almost limitless. Graphic designs, such as checks, plaids, and stripes have the most impact in this combination.

Color and pattern are also strongly identified with particular styles. A calico print, for instance, is an obvious choice for a casual country look, but most people would find it inappropriate for a formal decor. Thus, it is important to think about what associations a fabric has for you.

Balance is also a factor. When a room feels comfortable, it is usually the result of a harmonious relationship between color and pattern. Multi-colored patterns, such as paisleys, plaids, and florals, for example, infuse a space with energy, but can be overwhelming if used with a heavy hand.

Successfully mixing patterns also requires a common denominator. That means making sure patterns share a specific color or motif. If you are choosing a fabric to go with a floral print you already have,

try one that picks up a dominating shade in the pattern. Or, if your sofa fabric displays a cabbage-rose theme, you might choose pillow covers in a leaf pattern that complements the roses. A mix of busy patterns can be toned down with some solid colors.

Another factor to consider is how a fabric relates to the article of furniture you are covering. Are there special features to emphasize? For example, if a chair has elaborate cabriole legs that you intend to leave visible, you probably want to stay away from an ornate pattern that will compete. The fabric should also work with the shape of a piece. A solid color can emphasize the distinctive profile of a sofa or armchair, while a large repeating print might be cut off in odd ways on the curved arms or back of a sofa.

Finally, the style of a furniture piece itself should be taken into account. French toile, for example, would be appropriate for a French country armchair, while a homespun check would work for an early American wing chair.

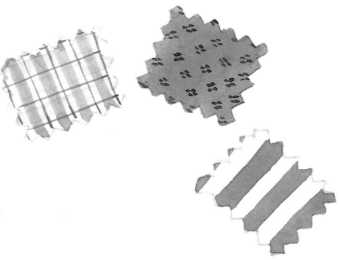

Sometimes furniture style suggests a fabric choice. A checked homespun suits an early American wing chair, while a delicate toile can look just right on a French Provincial piece.

buying fabric

Shopping for fabric is an endeavor that takes time, effort and inspiration. Even if you've done preliminary research, or kept a scrapbook, starting the actual search is likely to be bewildering. Whether you find yourself in a store, confronted with bolts of fabric stretching for aisle after aisle, or lost in a stack of swatch books, it's easy to succumb to sensory overload.

In the end, your choice should come at least partially from the heart. You do not have to stand in front of the bolt and debate its merits, or ask for second and third opinions. You will see it and you will love it—a case of instant attraction. Knowing that you instinctively love a fabric that also fulfills your color and pattern needs is surely a good reason to consider it a strong candidate for a purchase that is going to be in your home for a long time to come.

natural fibers

Practicality, however, must also enter into the decision. What is practical depends on fabric type, and in slipcovering, there is no question that pure natural fabrics yield the best results. Why? Because natural fabrics hold their shape, can be cleaned effectively, breathe well, feel pleasant, and last.

Of all natural fibers, cotton is by far the most versatile for slipcovers. It is cool and smooth, and because it absorbs dye so successfully it is available in an enormous range of colors and patterns. Cotton also gathers and creases well, so it can be adapted to almost any slipcover style.

Depending on the weight of the fabric and how your furniture piece is to be used, recommended choices in the cotton family include ticking, broadcloth, corduroy, canvas, calico, chino, duck, muslin, sailcloth, poplin, and denim, as well as cotton velveteens and damasks. The extra body of polished cotton, chintz, cotton sateen, and cotton taffeta makes these glazed fabrics good candidates as well.

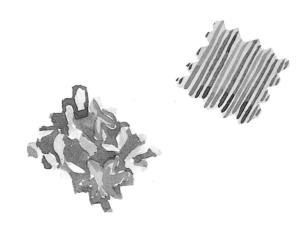

In the natural category, linen too is favored for covering furniture, not only for its durability, but also for the smooth, comfortable feeling the fabric takes on with time and repeated washings. Its cool, fresh look makes linen a traditional choice for summer slipcovers, offering a seasonal alternative to the heavier, sometimes scratchy materials used for upholstery. Linen, however, is notoriously prone to wrinkling, so it generally works best for loose, casual slipcover styles.

Silk is another possibility, although best limited to pillows because it doesn't hold up to daily wear or exposure to sunlight, and can also develop runs. The more durable silk-and-cotton or silk-and-linen blends are better used for coverings, but their slippery texture can make them difficult to sew.

While many wools are too scratchy and stretchy for slipcovers, wool flannel is a great choice because of its tighter weave and soft finish. The rich colors of a Scottish tartan will also warm a room, making a chair or sofa look cosy to curl up in.

upholstery fabrics

Heavy fabrics with a nap or pile, such as velvet, tapestries, brocades, and some corduroy fall into the upholstery-weight category, designed as they are to be tacked in place rather than stitched. They don't all have to be ruled out for slipcovering, however. Many medium- and lightweight corduroys and vel-

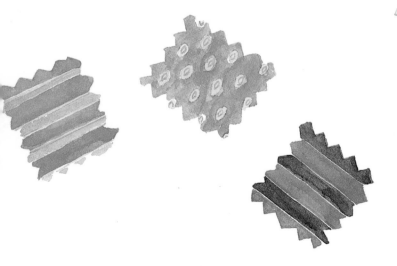

vets, for example, can be seamed, as can many brocades and tapestries. Moreover, their interesting textures, rich colors, and heavier feel can give a slipcover the richer look of upholstery.

bed linens

Among the other excellent sources for slipcover fabric are ready-made bed linens. But bed sheets should be quilted because they do not have enough body on their own to hold their shape or wear well (see Chapter Six, pages 128–131.) In general sheets are a good buy because they offer a lot of yardage for the dollar, and often come trimmed with welting, ruffles and borders that can be incorporated in your slipcover.

Bed sheets offer a surprising array of patterns that work well for slipcovers, including plaids, stripes, and florals.

Look for sheets in 100% cotton with a 200-thread count, which ensures a good, tight weave. (Both fiber content and thread count should be marked on the packages.) Cotton flannels are particularly desirable for their soft texture.

Thin flannel blankets of pure cotton or wool are good candidates as are woven cotton bedspreads with an overall pattern.

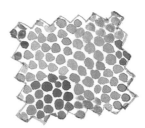

Simple motifs like polka dots take on strikingly different moods depending on their size, color, and background.

vintage fabrics

If they are in good condition, vintage fabrics should not be overlooked. Old drapery panels can be excellent for slipcovering and are likely to be in better shape than tablecloths and bedspreads—although these too may be cut into pieces for smaller projects, such as pillow covers. Drapery panels are often found in widths approximating those of bolt fabric, and usually in lengths substantial enough to cover a large piece of furniture. Moreover, drapery panels are sometimes double-lined with a flannel interlining, very expensive to duplicate today, which can be removed and reused.

synthetics

As a rule of thumb, it is best to avoid pure synthetics, which generally don't have the resilience to stand up to constant wear. With a few cleanings, slipcovers of dacron, polyester, nylon, acrylic, rayon,

and other synthetics will sag, bag, pucker, tear, fade, pill, and generally disappoint. And that's not all—sitting on a slipcover of synthetic fiber can make you feel hot and sticky. Synthetics, however, are sometimes available in blends with natural fibers, and if the synthetic constitutes no more than 40 per cent of the overall fiber content, the fabric can probably work for a slipcover.

Because some synthetics are especially convincing, it is not always easy to tell by sight or feel whether or not a fabric is woven of natural fibers. You can usually trust a label if there is one, but some stores, particularly bargain outlets, are happy to pass off a synthetic for pure cotton or linen.

If you have any doubts, break off a few long threads from the fabric you are considering. Place them in an ashtray and set a match (*not* a cigarette lighter) to them. Natural fibers burn quickly, with a clean blue flame and a woody odor. Linen fibers leap into flame and are quickly reduced to gray ash. Cotton fibers burn more slowly and leave a darker ash. By contrast, synthetic fibers melt, and the match flame is quickly extinguished. If you have to keep lighting matches to get the threads to burn, and if they emit a chemical-like odor, you can be sure the fabric has a synthetic content.

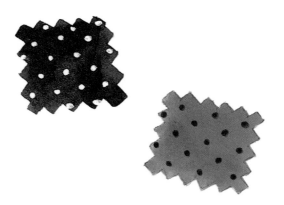

lining fabric

Most slipcovers require some sort of lining, although it is usually limited to the skirt. If your fabric is at all see-through, you will need to line all the pieces. Among the best fabrics to use for lining are bed sheets (you will need a supply on hand anyway for making your patterns.) In this case, the sheets can be a synthetic blend, since the lining will not show. If you desire heavier lining, unbleached muslin is an economical alternative. You can also use polished cotton, or light-weight flannel. Try to buy your lining in the same width as your fabric.

Stripes will accentuate the lines of a chair and generally look best when run vertically.

The classic combination of black-and-white has infinite varieties, and often yields a bold, graphic effect. Two different patterns used on the same slipcover can be particularly eye-catching.

fabric weights

No matter how beautiful the color, attractive the pattern, or excellent the quality, your fabric won't be suitable if it does not have the right weight.

Any knowledgeable salesperson can offer advice on this subject, but there is also a simple test you can perform yourself. Feel the fabric between your thumb and fingers. If it is thinner than a bed sheet, it will not be appropriate for most slipcovers, although it might work for a loose, decorative drape, such as the transparent styles shown in Chapter One. Also, put your hand behind a layer of the fabric as it lies on the bolt. If you can see the outline of your hand, the yardage will be too thin, unless lined or quilted.

Fabric can also be too heavy. Much upholstery yardage, for example, is too thick to sew together in the layers a seam and welting require. In the end, your choice will be limited to what your sewing

machine can handle. If you are considering a heavy fabric, ask for a swatch, or buy a half yard. Put four layers together and try stitching them on your machine, adjusting the tension appropriately. If you can sew through all four layers, the fabric is a candidate for a slipcover without welting, or one with welting but no skirt. If you can stitch through six layers, the fabric will work for a slipcover with both welting and a skirt. If only two layers can be sewn, the fabric won't be suitable for a large project, but instead could be used for a pillow cover with no welting.

fabric widths

The most commonly used widths for slipcover fabrics are 48″, and 54″–60″, measured selvage to

where to find fabric

Aside from a large department store, slipcover fabric can be found in any retail outlet catering to the home sewer. It can also be ordered from swatches at paint and wallpaper stores, and at some home furnishing enterprises. Businesses that deal in slipcovering and upholstery offer fabric as well, but they may not be willing to do so independently of their sewing services.

Interior decorators are another source. Like upholsterers, many will not want to be bothered with a customer who doesn't need their full services. They can, however, open the door to the world of "To the Trade," from which the ordinary retail customer is barred.

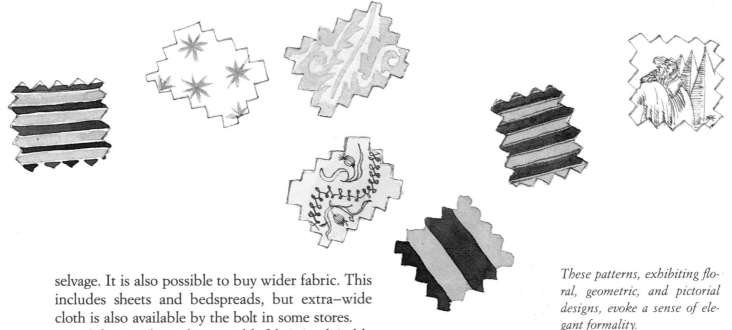

selvage. It is also possible to buy wider fabric. This includes sheets and bedspreads, but extra–wide cloth is also available by the bolt in some stores.

Selecting the widest possible fabric is advisable for three reasons. It will nearly always be a better buy per square yard, it will accommodate ruffles and skirting without the need for extra yardage, and it will help prevent the need for piecing when covering large areas.

If you are using a 48″–wide fabric to cover a sofa that is 60″ wide, for example, you will need more than one piece for the back, unless you run the yardage horizontally in a process called railroading (see Chapter Six, page 131.)

These patterns, exhibiting floral, geometric, and pictorial designs, evoke a sense of elegant formality.

If you are interested in a particular fabric design you have seen in a decorating magazine, check to see if the manufacturer is identified. To-the-Trade textile houses are often listed in the back-page buying guides, sometimes with an 800-number. In most cases, you will not be able to order directly from the textile house, but dialing the 800-number will put you in touch with a local retailer, such as a home furnishings store, that can order for you.

bargains

Cut-rate quality fabrics can often be found at mill-end fabric stores, where "seconds" and surplus bolts of fabric are sold in job lots. Beware, however. Bargain stores offer good deals, but also lots of junk.

If you don't really know your fabric, bring along someone who does, or buy a yard and experiment with it. Don't purchase fabric off a bolt that is almost empty, because the next bolt may have not gone through the same dye lot. Make sure you examine every inch of the yardage on both sides to catch any irregularities in the weave, color or printing.

Finally, don't overlook antique stores, flea markets, yard and estate sales, and second-hand shops. Here you might find vintage draperies and tablecloths, and old fabric still on the bolt. These can be the best discoveries of all.

a note on trims

Edgings, ribbons, cording, and other trims come in an enormous assortment of colors and designs, but there are essentially only two different types: dressmaker's and drapery. As a rule, it is best to avoid dressmaker's trim. Because it is intended for clothing, it is not as durable as drapery trim and tends to be more expensive. The number of yards needed for a slipcover can add up surprisingly fast.

Antique trims are also an option. Good drapery trim of silk, wool, or cotton ages particularly well and often outlasts the fabric it was intended to decorate. It can be found in perfect condition, still attached to an otherwise unusable piece of cloth.

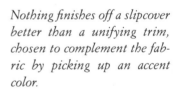

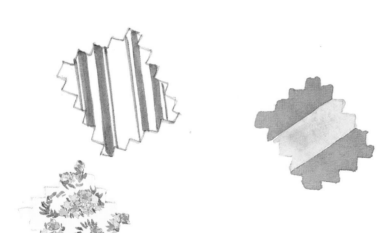

Nothing finishes off a slipcover better than a unifying trim, chosen to complement the fabric by picking up an accent color.

getting started

The key to sewing a successful slipcover lies in good preparations. Before you start, make time to put everything in order and to set up a clean, clutter-free work space where you have enough room to cut, iron, and sew. And don't take short cuts. Measuring and pattern making may seem tedious, but they are well worth extra time and effort. By the time you get to sewing the actual slipcover, the job will be almost done.

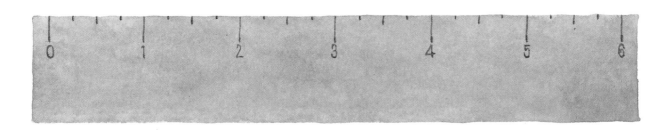

sewing supplies

When buying and organizing supplies for sewing a slipcover, one rule applies: have enough on hand and have it all. The middle of a project is no time to find out that you have forgotten your interfacing or have run out of buttons.

The checklist of supplies at right is designed to help you take inventory. Most items can be found at hardware, department, fabric, or dime stores.

establishing a work space

An organized and well-stocked work space is essential to any successful sewing project. You need to allow room not only for the piece of furniture you are covering, but also for the work table, ironing board, loose cushions and pillows, and the fabric itself. It is important to have ample clearance on all four sides of the furniture piece, since you are going to be making many trips around it as you measure, make patterns, and fit the cover.

A good work table is also a necessity. A kitchen or dining table makes an excellent work surface, if you are not worried about cutting on it. Next best is a sheet of muslin–covered plywood—4′ × 8′ is a good size—set over a table or desk. Wherever you work, be sure to clean the floor thoroughly. That way you do not have to be concerned about soiling the fabric that will inevitably spill onto the floor as you are cutting, draping, and ironing.

preparing the furniture

Strip the cushions and any existing covers off the furniture piece and vacuum all the surfaces, using a nozzle attachment to go deep into the crevices. Remove any loose staples with pliers, and using a small hammer, tap loose nails back into the frame. Add more 1″ brads or headless nails if necessary. Trim frayed threads and slipstitch torn areas closed; spot clean any stains.

checklist

sewing materials

- ☐ Fabric
- ☐ Fringe or other trim
- ☐ Batting for padding (cotton or polyester fiber)
- ☐ Sheets or muslin for patterns, skirt lining, and deck
- ☐ Interfacing
- ☐ Foam for cushions
- ☐ Welting cord
- ☐ Thread—at least four large spools (use contrasting thread for basting)
- ☐ Cloth tape measure
- ☐ T-pins
- ☐ Dressmaker's pins and pin cushion
- ☐ Sewing needles: all-purpose sharps, short quilting needle, curved upholstery needle
- ☐ Sewing machine needles: #11–#14 (75-90) for light- to mediumweight fabric; and #16–#18 (100-110) for heavier weight fabric
- ☐ Tracer's wheel and carbon paper
- ☐ Tailor's pencil
- ☐ Sewing machine attachments: zipper foot, ruffler, quilting foot
- ☐ Zippers, Velcro™, snaps
- ☐ Shirring tape

household items

- ☐ Steam iron and ironing board
- ☐ Pressing cloth
- ☐ Spray mister
- ☐ Roll of brown wrapping paper at least 24″ wide
- ☐ Index cards
- ☐ Electronic pocket calculator
- ☐ Yardstick
- ☐ Ruler with ¼″ marks (see-through plastic)
- ☐ T-square or right angle (see-through plastic)
- ☐ #2 pencils and sharpener

hardware

- ☐ Small claw hammer
- ☐ Pliers
- ☐ Staple gun and staples
- ☐ Sewing shears: 5″ blades or longer
- ☐ Small sharp-tipped scissors for clipping
- ☐ 1″ wire brads or small headless nails

padding

Padding a seating piece is optional, but it will make a hard sofa or chair softer and more resilient. It also absorbs puckers and wrinkles, giving a slipcover a snug fit, and provides a smooth surface over channeled or buttoned upholstery. Use polyester batting, which is sold in sheets. This can be cut into pieces that fit over the back, arms, and cushions. There is no need to pin; the batting will cling to the chair on its own.

determining yardage needs

The next step is to figure yardage. Obviously, to avoid overbuying fabric, you will want to determine exactly how much you need. If you're not worried about extra expense, a general estimate should be fine. But if you are savings-conscious, you will want to know to the very inch not how much but how *little* fabric to buy.

The scale-size yardage strips on pages 70–75 will help you arrive at a more precise yardage estimate. To use them, you need to measure your furniture piece—a process that will be required for pattern making anyway. Each yardage strip, drawn to the scale of $\frac{1}{4}'' = 10''$, represents a 10-yard length of fabric; one is 48″ wide, the other 54″–60″ wide—the recommended widths for slipcover fabric. There are also layout schemes for standard-size bed linens.

Finally, you will find formulas for calculating skirting and repeats, and a chart showing ballpark yardage estimates for fabric, as well as for welting and trim, skirting, batting, and extras.

To use the layout strips, follow the directions on pages 64–68 to measure your furniture piece. According to these measurements, you will then cut simple scale-size patterns from index cards that can be placed directly on a blank layout strip and arranged to show how much yardage the full-size pattern pieces will take up.

measuring

Before you begin measuring, have on hand a cloth tape measure, a pad and pencil, a ruler with $\frac{1}{4}''$ markings, and a few index cards.

You will be measuring major sections of a furniture piece: (A) the back, (B) the arms, (C) the front, and (D-E) the seat and back cushions. For some furniture you need to measure (F) the seat or deck, or (T) the top. You will also note down (P) the perimeter, to calculate for skirting. Smaller slipcover sections such as the shoulders (the areas between the inside and outside arm), arm fronts, and extras such as arm protectors and wings do not have to be included in yardage estimates, because they can be cut from scraps. To save yardage, the deck (the area under the seat cushion) is covered in sheeting or muslin, except for a 4″ strip in front.

Each furniture section is measured with only a length and width dimension—even if it is an odd shape—so that all of your card cut-outs will be squares or rectangles. To make a drawing to the scale of $\frac{1}{4}'' = 10''$, simply tick off the $\frac{1}{4}''$ marks on a ruler using each $\frac{1}{4}''$ mark to represent 10″. (A 40″ measurement would equal four $\frac{1}{4}''$ marks, or 1″). Before you begin, remove all the cushions.

measuring an armchair, sofa, or chaise

An armchair, a sofa, and a chaise are all measured in the same manner. Essentially, they are the same piece of furniture: the only real difference is in the width, seat length, and number of cushions. The (C) front will be greatly extended on a chaise.

(A) back

1. *Length:* Start on the outside. For a skirtless slipcover, measure from the floor or leg tops, depending on where you want the skirt to stop. For a skirted slipcover, measure from the skirtline. Measure up, over, and down the inside back to the deck. Add 10″.

2. *Width:* Measure across the back at the widest point and halfway into the shoulder (if there is one). Add 6″.

3. Using a scale of $\frac{1}{4}'' = 10''$, draw a

square or rectangle to these two measurements on an index card. Make one cut-out to this size. Draw an arrow along the lengthwise edge and mark the length and width measurements and the letter A.

(B) arms

1. *Length:* Start on the outside. For a skirtless slipcover, begin measuring from the floor or leg tops. For a skirted slipcover, measure from the skirtline. Measure up, over, and down the inside of the arm to the deck. Add 10″.

2. *Width:* Measure from the arm front seam to the inside back of the furniture piece. Add 4″.

3. Using a scale of ¼″ = 10″, draw a square or rectangle to these two measurements on an index card. Make two cut-outs to this size. Draw an arrow along the lengthwise edges and mark the length and width measurements and the letter B on each.

(C) front

1. *Length:* For a skirtless slipcover, measure from the floor or leg tops. For a skirted slipcover, measure from the skirtline. Measure up to the front edge of the deck. Add 6″. (Add 2″ more if you are using foam padding on the deck.)

2. *Width:* Measure from arm seam to arm seam. Add 6″.

3. Using a scale of ¼″ = 10″, draw a square or rectangle to these two measurements on an index card. Make one cut-out to this size. Draw an arrow along the lengthwise edge and mark the length and width measurements and the letter C.

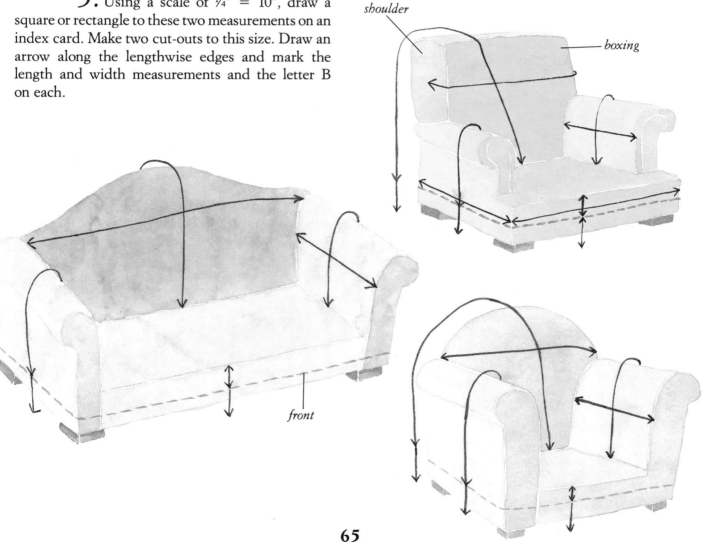

shoulder

boxing

front

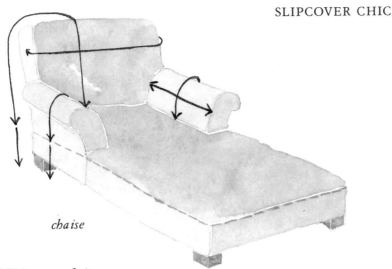

slipper chair

chaise

(D) cushions

1. *Length:* Measure from front to back, going half way into the boxing. Add 2″.

2. *Width:* Measure from side to side, going half way into the boxing. Add 2″.

3. Using a scale of ¼″ = 10″, draw a square or rectangle to these two measurements on an index card. Make two cut-outs to this size. Draw an arrow along the lengthwise edges and mark the length and width measurements and the letter D on each. Repeat for each seat cushion.

4. Repeat for each back cushion, if there are any. If the back cushions are a different size than the seat cushions, mark their cut-outs E.

(P) perimeter

Measure all the way around your piece at the skirtline, if there is one. Note this figure.

measuring a slipper chair

A slipper chair is a small armless chair with a skirt. Some have attached seats, others removable cushions.

slipper chair with an attached seat

(A) back

1. *Length:* Start on the outside. Begin at the skirtline. Measure up, over, and down the inside back to the seat. Add 1″.

2. *Width:* Measure across the back at the widest point and halfway into the shoulder if there is one. Add 1″.

3. Using a scale of ¼″ = 10″, draw a square or rectangle to these two measurements on an index card. Make one cut-out to this size. Draw an arrow along the lengthwise edge and mark the length and width measurements and the letter A.

Measuring Cushions

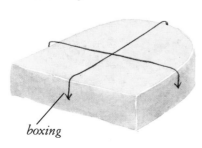

boxing

(F) seat

1. *Length:* Measure from the front skirtline to the inside back. Add 1″.

2. *Width:* Measure from side skirtline to side skirtline. Add 1″.

3. Using a scale of ¼″ = 10″, draw a square or rectangle to these two measurements on an index card. Make one cut-out to this size. Draw an arrow along the lengthwise edge and mark the length and width measurements and the letter F.

(P) perimeter

Measure all the way around the piece at the skirtline. Note down the figure.

slipper chair with a separate cushion

(A) back

Remove the cushion and follow Steps 1–3 for the slipper chair with an attached seat.

(D) cushion

Measure as for armchairs, sofas, and chaises.

(F) deck

1. *Length:* Start at the front. Measure from the front skirtline to the inside back. Add 1″.

2. *Width:* Measure from side skirtline to side skirtline. Add 1″.

3. Using a scale of ¼″ = 10″, draw a square or rectangle to these two measurements on an index card. Make one cut-out to this size. Draw an arrow along the lengthwise edge and mark the length and width measurements and the letter F.

(P) perimeter

Measure all the way around the piece at the skirtline, if there is one. Note this figure.

measuring a daybed

(D) cushion

Measure as for armchairs, sofas, and chaises.

(F) deck

1. *Length:* Measure from end skirtline to end skirtline. Add 1″.

2. *Width:* Measure from side skirtline to side skirtline. Add 1″.

3. Using a scale of ¼″ = 10″, draw a square or rectangle to these two measurements on an index card. Make one cut-out to this size. Draw an arrow along the lengthwise edge and mark the length and width measurements and the letter F.

(P) perimeter

Measure all the way around the piece at the skirtline. Note down the figure.

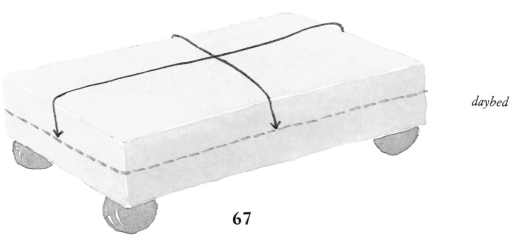

daybed

measuring an ottoman

square or rectangular ottoman

(T) top

1. *Length:* Measure from end skirtline to end skirtline. Add 1".

2. *Width:* Measure from side skirtline to side skirtline. Add 1."

3. Using a scale of ¼" = 10", draw a square or rectangle to these two measurements on an index card. Make one cut-out to this size. Draw an arrow along the lengthwise edge and mark the length and width measurements and the letter T.

(P) perimeter

Measure all the way around the piece at the skirtline. Note this figure.

round ottoman

(T) top

1. Measure the diameter from skirtline to skirtline and add 1". Using a scale of ¼" = 10", draw a circle to this diameter measurement on an index card. Make one cut-out to this size. Mark the letter T.

(P) perimeter

Measure all the way around the piece at the skirtline. Note this figure.

using the layout strips

Turn to the layout strips on pages 74–75. Place your cut-outs on one strip and move them around until you have found a way to lay them out using a minimum amount of yardage. (Sample layouts are provided on pages 70–73, showing how cut-outs for a two-seat sofa might be arranged. Your layout will probably look different.) Remember, you will need enough scraps to cut shoulders, facings, arm fronts, wings, arm protectors, and throw pillows. If it looks as though you will need to calculate additional fabric for these, see the chart on page 76.

If using a fabric with a directional pattern or nap (texture), be sure the arrows on your cutouts all follow the lengthwise edge of the layout strip. If using a fabric in a solid color or with a nondirectional pattern, your cutouts can be laid out either crosswise or lengthwise on the strip, or in a combination of the two.

Cutting out a fabric piece across the grain of the fabric is called "railroading" (see Chapter Six, page 131). Railroading works for non-directional patterns, since it makes no difference to the eye how the fabric is cut. However, because the lengthwise grain of the fabric is much stronger than the crosswise grain, slipcover sections that undergo stress, such as the back and arms, are best cut on the lengthwise grain.

It is also important to avoid cutting any two sections that will be seamed together on opposite grains. The section cut on the crosswise grain will stretch, while the section cut on the lengthwise grain will remain stable, so that one edge will come out longer than the other when they are stitched.

When the cut-outs are arranged on the layout

strip, use the scale to see how much fabric would be needed for that particular width of fabric. If you haven't chosen a fabric yet, estimate for both 48″ and 54″–60″ fabrics, so you can have both figures on hand when you go shopping.

skirts and skirt lining

Skirts and skirt linings require the same amount of yardage. The following formulas will help you determine exactly how much you need.

tailored skirt with kick pleats

Perimeter (P) plus 60″.

ruffled or box-pleated skirt

When using a directional pattern, a ruffled or box-pleated skirt will require several sections, since you must cut the sections from selvage to selvage. Therefore, they can only be as wide as the fabric itself.

To determine how many sections you need, multiply the (P) perimeter by 3. Divide that number by the width of the fabric. Then, measure the height of the skirt from floor to skirtline and add 2″. Multiply that number by the number of sections. Divide by 36 to determine the required yardage.

When using nondirectional fabrics, you can cut longer strips along the lengthwise grain. You may be able to cut at least some of these from your scraps.

welting

To calculate the yardage needed for welting cord, measure all the seams that you plan to welt and add 24″. To calculate yardage for the casing fabric (see Chapter Six, pages 139–140), use this table:

fabric amount	yield in running yards	
	48″ wide	54″–60″ wide
¼ yd	5 yds	6½ yds
½ yd	11 yds	13 yds
1 yd	22 yds	26 yds

repeats

To estimate the additional yardage needed for a fabric pattern with repeats (see Chapter Six, page 131) measure the lengthwise distance between the repeat. Double that number and multiply it by the number of yards you have already estimated on the layout strip. For example, if the fabric estimate is 6 yards and the repeat is 6″, add 72″.

bed linens

You can also use bed linens for fabric. Before you buy, consider the total yardage you will need. Two twin-size bedspreads, for example, yield close to 1½ yards more than one king-size bedspread. Similarly, two twin-size sheets yield a yard more than one king-size and can cost less.

If the pattern layout does not leave enough scrap fabric to cut out the small sections, you can get extra fabric from standard size pillow cases. Unseamed, each case yields slightly less than a square yard of fabric. If you use bed sheets, remember that you will need to quilt some sections (see Chapter Six, pages 128–131).

how to scrimp

- Use a solid or nondirectional fabric without a nap
- Use fabric that is 60″ or wider.
- Make more, smaller slipcover sections. Piece small sections from scraps and camouflage the seams with quilting.
- Eliminate the skirt.
- Make the bottom of seat cushions out of lining fabric.
- Before you buy your fabric, follow all the steps for making patterns. You will then have accurate finished dimensions and can use the patterns themselves to calculate yardage.
- Use contrasting welting.
- Railroad.

sample layout for a two-seat sofa

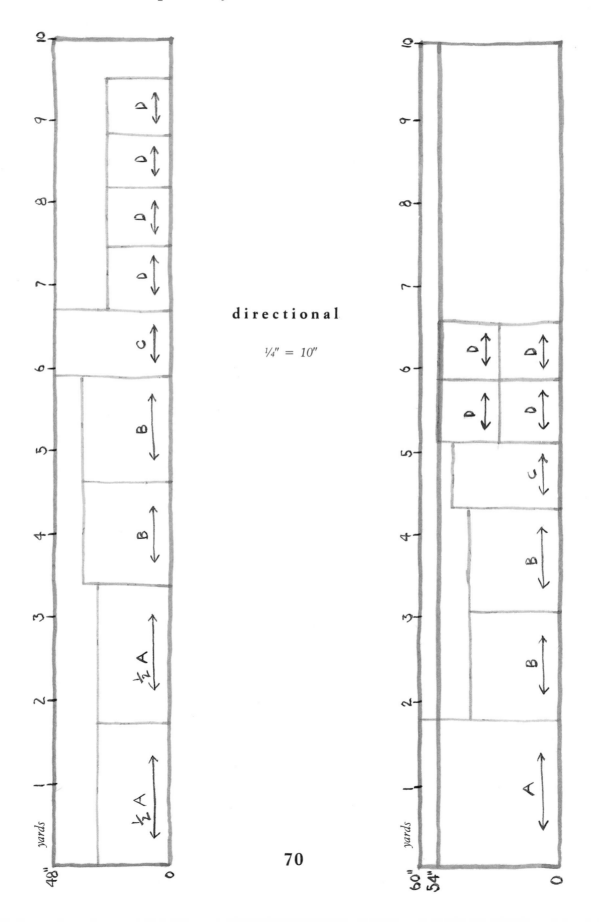

directional

¼″ = 10″

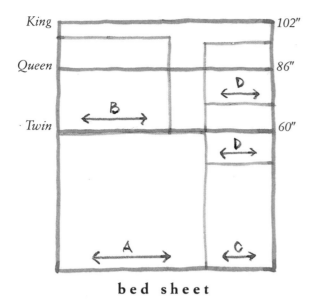

bed sheet

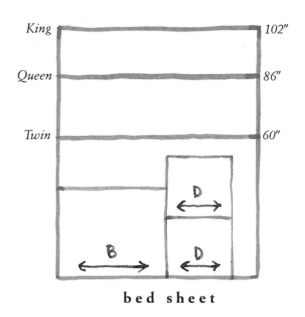

bed sheet

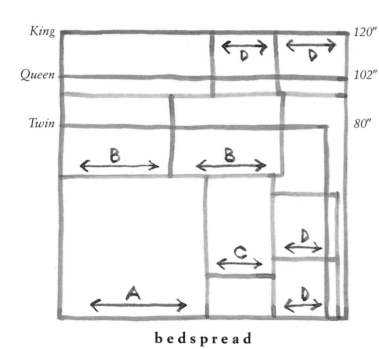

bedspread

directional layout

As a rule of thumb, a directional layout will take up the most yardage because most sections won't fit side by side. The scheme above shows how the sections for a two-seat sofa could be placed on one king-size sheet and one twin-size sheet.

sample layout for a two-seat sofa

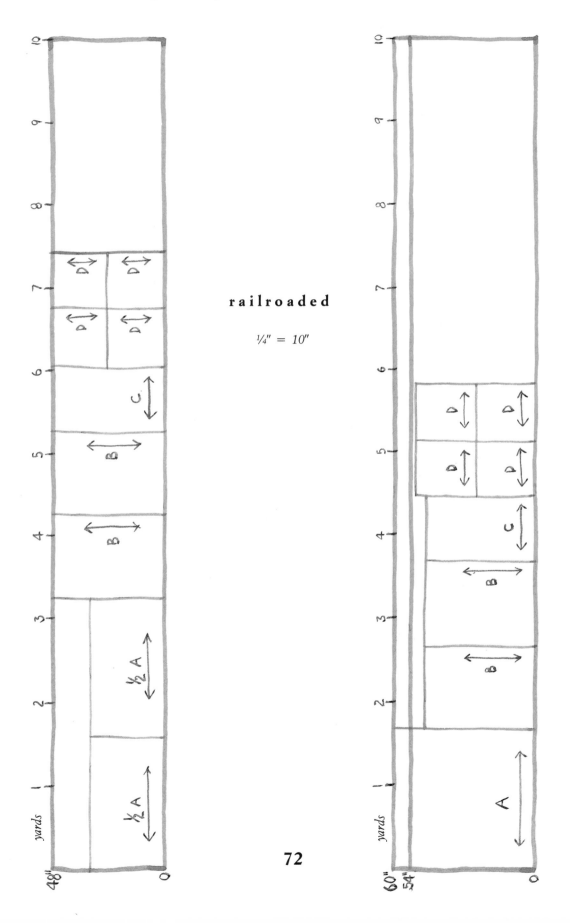

railroaded

¼" = 10"

72

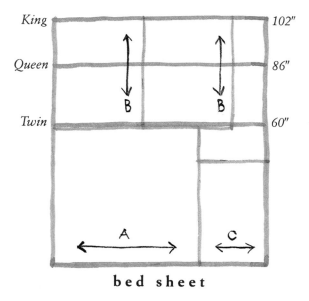

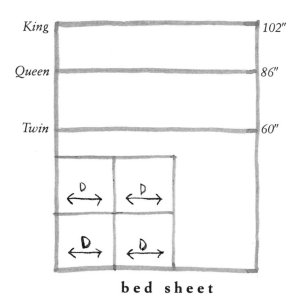

bed sheet

bed sheet

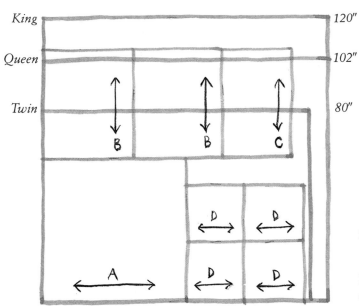

bedspread

railroaded layout

A railroaded layout will usually take up less yardage than a directional layout because the slip-cover sections can be turned sideways on the fabric.

sample layout

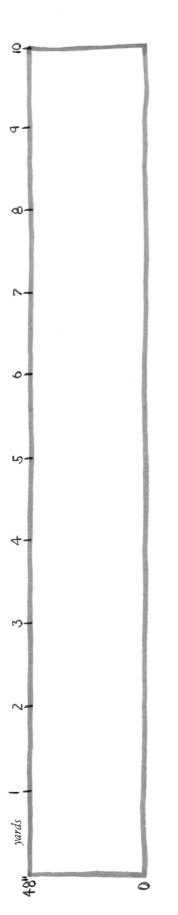

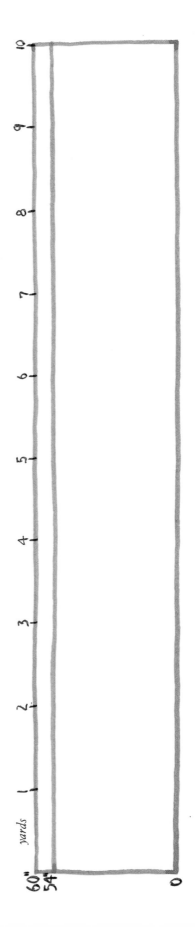

$\frac{1}{4}'' = 10''$

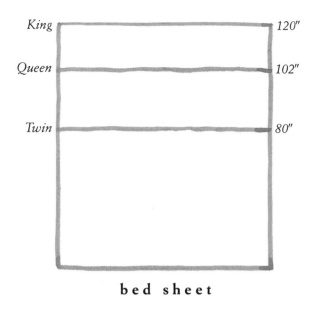

b e d   s h e e t

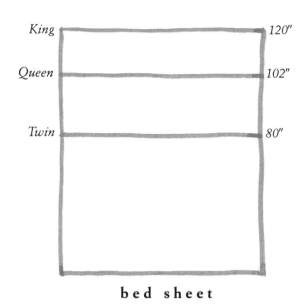

b e d   s h e e t

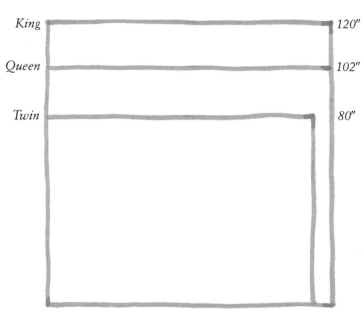

b e d s p r e a d

s a m p l e   l a y o u t

Use these strips to arrange your scale-size card cut-outs to see how much fabric would be required for bed linens and different yardage widths.

estimating yardage

		armchair		slipper chair		love seat		two-seat sofa		three-seat sofa		chaise		daybed		ottoman	
yardage *(inches wide)*		48	54-60	48	54-60	48	54-60	48	54-60	48	54-60	48	54-60	48	54-60	48	54-60
fabric for sections A, B, C, D *(Does not include skirting, back cushions, or extras)*	railroaded	7½ yds	4½ yds	2 yds	2 yds	8 yds	7½ yds	7½ yds	6 yds	12 yds	10 yds	5 yds	2½ yds	5 yds	2½ yds	2 yds	1 yd
	directional	8 yds	4½ yds	2 yds	2 yds	8 yds	7½ yds	10 yds	7½ yds	14 yds	12 yds	13 yds	6 yds	5 yds	2½ yds	2 yds	1 yd
	bed sheet	1 king, 1 twin		1 twin		1 king, 1 twin		1 king, 1 twin		2 queen, 1 twin		1 king, 1 twin		1 king, 1 twin		1 twin	
	bedspread	2 twin		1 twin		1 king		1 king		3 twin		1 twin		1 twin		1 twin	
batting *(81" × 96" sheet)*		1 sheet		1 sheet		1 sheet		2 sheets		3 sheets		1 sheet		1 sheet		1 sheet	
cord *(running yardage for full welting)*		17 yds		4 yds		18 yds		33 yds		47 yds		22 yds		16 yds		8 yds	

extras

Back cushions: 1 yard each
Throw pillows: ½ yard each
Arm protectors: ½ yard per pair
Extra arm fronts: ½ yard per pair
Small sections: 1 yard

tally sheet

Total fabric for
   sections A, B, C, and D   ———

Skirt   ———

Back cushions E   ———

Small sections   ———

Welting casing strips   ———

Repeats   ———

Throw pillows   ———

Arm protectors   ———

Extra arm fronts   ———

TOTAL YARDAGE   ———

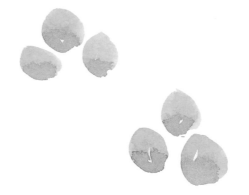

cats

Cats have a way of using arm fronts as scratching posts. If you cut extra arm fronts, you can replace them should a pet cause damage. Carefully remove the existing arm front, snipping the stitches using small sharp-tipped scissors, and replace with the extras.

testing the fabric

Before you make your final purchase, it is critical to test the fabric you are considering for shrinkage and colorfastness. Many fabrics sold today are already pre-shrunk, but to be safe, consider any length of fabric a mystery until you have put it through a trial run.

pre-shrinking

Shrinkage is not necessarily bad, for it makes a fabric weave tighter and stronger. You just don't want it to occur *after* you have made your slipcover. Check the selvages and the label on the bolt for cleaning directions. If the fabric has not been pre-shrunk by the manufacturer, or if the label indicates it will shrink more than 1%, you will need to pre-shrink it yourself.

dry cleaning

On some yardage, the words "Dry Clean Only" are clearly printed on the selvages. Other fabric may not be marked with cleaning instructions, but if it has a treated surface, such as on chintz or damask, it should also be dry cleaned.

To test, buy a ½-yard sample of the fabric you are considering and carefully measure it from selvage edge to selvage edge. Send it out to be dry cleaned, and when it comes back, measure it again. If it has shrunk, you will need to have the entire length of fabric dry cleaned before you cut into it.

Even after dry cleaning, some fabric will continue to shrink. To determine if this will happen, mist your sample until damp, and steam press it with a very hot iron until it is fully dry. Measure again. If it has shrunk more than ⅛" you will need to account for this when you cut the fabric.

machine washing

Washable fabrics can take their test drive in the washer and dryer. Measure the ½-yard sample as above, and launder it with the washer on the hottest setting. Tumble dry the sample on the hottest setting until it is completely dry. Measure the sample again.

If it has shrunk, all of the yardage will need to be pre-shrunk.

When you launder your sample, check for sizing as well. Sized fabrics are not recommended for slipcovering because the sizing will rinse out and the fabric will lose its sheen. If there is scum in the rinse water and the sample comes out limp and lifeless, you will not want to use the fabric.

When you test washable fabric for shrinkage, you will also find out how colorfast it is. If the colors fade or bleed, the fabric will need to be dry cleaned. Any washable fabric becomes more colorfast if you dampen it and steam press it on the wrong side with a hot iron until it is completely dry.

preparing fabric for cutting

Pre-shrink the entire yardage according to your test results, either by sending it to the dry cleaners or by laundering. A large amount of yardage, as for a three-seat sofa, cannot be put into the washer in one length, but will need to be cut in two or more pieces. In this case, check your layout strip and cut-outs to see where the yardage can be cut. Make sure that one fabric piece is long enough to accommodate the back, arms, and front.

lining and notions

Lining made from bed sheets does not need to be pre-shrunk. Many launderings will have done that already. However, lining made of newly purchased muslin or other cotton should be pre-shrunk. It is also a good idea to mist and pre-shrink zippers with metal teeth using a hot steam iron. Run welting cord through the washer and hot dryer; coil the length of cord and tie it with a knot to secure it during the drying process.

squaring the edges and straightening the grain

Most likely, when your fabric was cut from the bolt, it was not cut evenly along the crosswise grain. This cutting edge must be trimmed perpendicular to the selvages.

Do this when the fabric is fresh from the dry cleaners or from the dryer. (If you are working with linen, mist it until damp, roll it tightly, and wrap it in a plastic bag to let the fibers soften for a few hours before proceeding. Steam press it dry.) Fold the fabric lengthwise with the right sides together, holding the selvage edges between your fingers. Shake out the wrinkles. Smooth the surface until the fold lies flat, and pin the selvages together. Using your table edge or a T-square, square off the cut edges.

When the fabric is squared, keep the right sides together and pin every 6″ along the entire length, shaking the cloth frequently to keep the fold line smooth and even. If the fold does not lie smoothly but keeps forming wrinkles on the bias, the grain is not straight (see Chapter Six, page 128). Grab the selvages in one hand and the fold in the other and pull the fabric in the opposite direction to the way the wrinkles are forming. Keep pulling the fabric and smoothing to the fold as you steam press. This will straighten the grain.

steam pressing

With the fabric still folded with the right sides together, steam press on both sides of the fold to crease it well. This fold can be used as a lengthwise grid line when the pattern pieces are laid out. If your fabric is 100% cotton or linen, mist it and steam press until it is dry. If the fabric contains any synthetic fibers, or if you are working with wool or a silk blend, use the cotton setting on your iron and a dampened pressing cloth. When working with chintz or other fabrics with a sheen or a raised surface, always steam press on the wrong side.

Leave the selvages intact, as they will become useful indicators of the lengthwise grain. Fold the fabric neatly and keep it that way until you are ready to lay out your patterns.

pattern making

Slipcovering has been known to reduce normally sanguine people to tears—an outcome that can avoided by making cloth patterns before you ever cut into your fabric. Pattern making eliminates confusion—and mistakes—and also ensures a good fit. Cloth patterns are only necessary, however, for armchairs, sofas, and chaises; slipper chairs, daybeds, ottomans, cushions and skirts do not require patterns, because these pieces do not present the fitting problems of furniture with arms. (See individual projects in Chapter Five.)

Bed sheets are great to use for cutting patterns; you can also use muslin. The cloth is cut into large blocks, which are pinned one at a time over the back, arms, front, and small areas until the furniture piece is covered. The patterns are then clipped to fit smoothly over the contours, smoothed, re-pinned, then basted together and trimmed to make a mock slipcover. Finally, each pattern is marked for cutting and sewing.

why make cloth patterns?

 Without a pattern, you will be making irrevocable cuts in your yardage before you really know what you are doing.

 Unlike paper patterns, cloth patterns can be pinned to one another, making it possible to accurately determine seam line placement.

 If you are slipcovering over dark upholstery, the patterns can be stitched to form an underlining that is slipped over the chair before the slipcover is put on.

 Cloth patterns hold up well and can be reused.

 Cloth patterns can be used as backing pieces for quilted slipcover sections.

determining the skirtline

If you do not want a skirt, the bottom edge of your pattern blocks will be placed so they fall to the bottom edge of the furniture piece or the top of the legs with an additional 2″ for fitting. If you are making a skirt, your pattern blocks will be placed so they fall only to the skirtline. Placement of the skirtline is a matter of personal preference; it can fall directly from the deck, or from any point below.

With your eye, decide where you want the skirt to fall from and mark with a pin. Using a yardstick, measure up from the floor to the pin. Using that measurement, mark the skirtline with a pin every few inches all the way around the furniture piece.

cutting pattern blocks

After you have cut each block, you will need to steam press a grid into it. To do so, fold the piece in half, then in half the other way. Steam press the creases. Fold it in half again, then again the other way. Steam press again. Unfold the cloth.

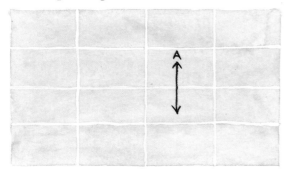

FIGURE 1
one-piece back

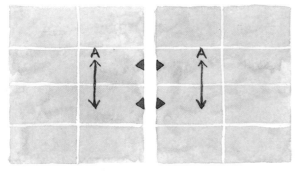

FIGURE 2
one-piece back with center seam

(A) back

One-piece Back: A one-piece back goes from the deck of the chair up to the top, then over and down to the bottom of the back. Cut a pattern block according to the measurements on your scale-size cut-out (A). Steam press the grid and transfer the directional arrow and letter from the cut-out (Figure 1).

Two-piece Back: If the top of the back is curved, or if you want a seam line or boxing across the top, you will need to cut the back into two pieces, an inside back and an outside back, connected by the seam or boxing.

Add an additional 4″ to the length measurement on the card cut-out. Cut a pattern block to the new measurements. Place the pattern block over the furniture back as for the one-piece back. With a pencil, mark a line on the pattern across the top of the furniture back. Remove the pattern block and cut it in two pieces along the marked line allowing 2 extra inches for fitting. Label one section "outside" and one section "inside" and mark notches on the tops where the sections will be seamed to each other or to a top boxing section. Steam press the grid and transfer the directional arrows and letters to each.

One-piece Back with Center Seam: If the back of the furniture piece is wider than your fabric, you will have to seam the fabric down the middle unless you are railroading (Figure 2).

Add 1″ to the width measurement on the (A) cut-out. Cut a pattern block according to the new measurements. Steam press the grid and cut the pattern down the center fold line. Label the two pattern sections A-1 and A-2, and pencil in notches where they will be seamed. Transfer the directional arrow.

Two-piece Back with Center Seam: Cut and label sections A-1 and A-2 for the inside back following the instructions for a one-piece back. Repeat for the outside back, marking the sections "A-1 outside" and "A-2 outside."

Channeled or Barrel Back: If the inside back has a deep curve or channeling, you will need to cover it with several pattern pieces (see page 81). Place a piece of sheeting over the inside back and trace the channel. Extend the line 1″ on the sides and 4″ at the bottom for the deck overlap. Cut out the piece and repeat for all the channels. Transfer the directional arrows and letter marks to each. Cut the outside back as for a two-piece back.

For a barrel back chair, follow the same process, cutting as many sections as you need to go around the curve.

pin-fitting the (A) back

One-piece Back: Measure to the center of the sofa or chair back and mark it with a pin. Place the pattern block over the back, matching the pin mark and the center crease line. Pin to secure (Figure 1).

Secure the edges of the pattern with T-pins. Place the 4″ overlap (tuck-in) at the bottom flat on the deck. Pin the bottom edge of the outside back to the bottom edge or to the skirtline of the furniture piece, leaving 2″ for fitting. Trim the pattern block leaving 2″ on the sides for fitting.

Two-piece Back with no Boxing: Measure to the outside center of the furniture back and mark it with a pin. Place the outside back pattern block over the furniture back, matching the pin mark and the center crease line. Pin to secure (Figure 2).

Place the inside back pattern block over the inside furniture back. Place the 4″ overlap (tuck-in) at the bottom flat on the deck. Pin the two patterns together at the top, matching the crease lines and notches. If the back is curved, the allowances will be uneven. Leave them that way for now.

For a skirtless cover, pin the bottom edge of the outside pattern block to the bottom edge of the furniture piece. For a skirted cover, pin outside at the skirtline, leaving 2″ for fitting.

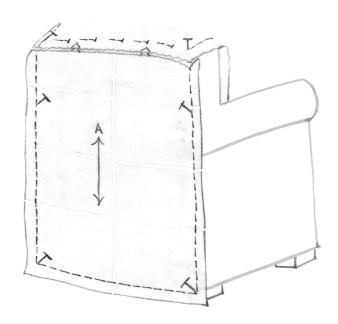

FIGURE 2

pin-fitting a two-piece back

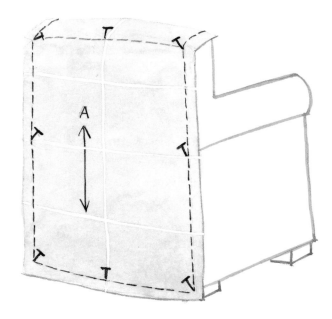

FIGURE 1

pin-fitting a one-piece back

Two-piece Back with Boxing: Follow the directions for the two-piece back with no boxing. Leave a 2″ fitting allowance at the top of the inside back and outside back pattern blocks (Figure 3). You will make a pattern for the boxing later.

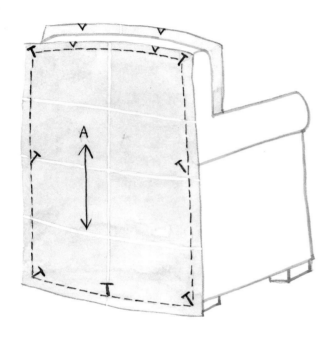

FIGURE 3
pin-fitting a two-piece back with boxing

One-piece Back with Center Seam: Place pattern blocks A-1 and A-2 with their right sides together and pin along the seam line, matching the creases and notches. Open the pattern block and place it over the furniture back with the seam line running down the middle. Pin-fit following the directions for a one-piece back.

Two-piece Back with Center Seam: Place pattern blocks A-1 "inside" and A-2 "inside" with their right sides together, and pin along the seam line, matching the creases and notches. Repeat for the "outside" pattern blocks. Open the pattern blocks and place them over the inside and outside back of the furniture piece, with the seam lines running down the middle. Pin-fit following the instructions for the two-piece back.

Channeled or Barrel Back: Measure to the outside center of the furniture back and mark it with a pin. Place the outside back pattern block over the back, matching the pin mark and the center crease line. Pin to secure.

Place the inside channels or barrel sections over the inside back, laying the 4″ overlaps (tuck-ins) out on the deck (Figure 4). Pin until they lie smoothly.

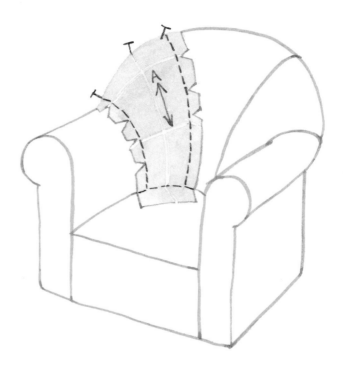

FIGURE 4
pin-fitting a channel back

(B)   a r m s

The shape of the arms will determine whether you can cover them in one or two pieces.

One-piece Arms: If the arms are not scrolled or curve only slightly, you can make a one-piece arm. Cut two pattern blocks according to the measurements on the scale-size cut-out (B). Steam press the grid and transfer the directional arrows and letters.

Two-piece Arms: If the arms are scrolled, extended,

or have top boxing, you will need to cut each pattern into an inside and an outside section. Add 4″ to the length measurement on your cut-outs and cut two pattern blocks to the new measurements. Place the pattern blocks over the arms as for the one-piece arms. With a pencil, mark a line along the center top of each arm from the inside back to the front. Remove the pattern blocks and cut them in two pieces along the line allowing 2 extra inches for fitting. Label the two sections for each arm "outside" and "inside," and mark notches on the tops where the sections will be seamed to each other or to a top boxing section. Steam press the grids and transfer the directional arrows and letter marks.

pin-fitting the (B) arms

One-piece Arms: Measure to the center of the outside arms from back to front and mark them with a pin. Place the pattern blocks over the arms, matching the pin mark and the center crease line.

Secure the edges of the pattern with T-pins. Lay the 4″ overlaps (tuck-ins) at the bottom flat on the deck. Pin the bottom edge of the outside arms to the bottom edges or skirtline of the furniture, leaving 2″ for fitting. Trim the patterns leaving 2″ on the sides for fitting.

Two-piece Arms (Moderate Scroll): For a moderate scroll you can follow the contours of the seam line close to the outside of the arms. Place each inside arm pattern over the curve of the arm and lay the 4″ overlap (tuck-in) on the deck. Pin the other edge of each inside arm at the seam line under the curve, leaving a 2″ fitting allowance (Figure 1). Clip.

Secure the bottom edge of each outside arm pattern to the bottom edge or skirtline of the furniture with T-pins. Pin the inside and outside arm patterns together at the seam line under the curve as shown, matching the creases and notches.

Two-piece Arms (Deep Scroll): For a deep scroll, you need to determine how far you can follow the contours of the arms and still be able to remove the finished slipcover.

Pin and trim the inside and outside arm sec-

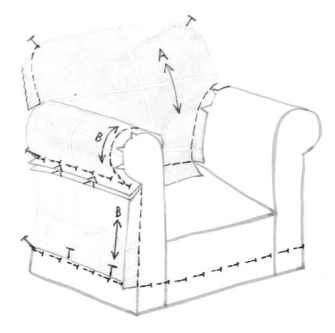

FIGURE 1
pin-fitting a two-piece arm

tions as for the moderate scroll. Try to remove the arm pieces gently. If the pieces cannot be slipped off because the pinned seam is too deep under the curve of the arm, re-pin them at a point higher up on the curve of the scroll, adjusting until they can be slipped off. There will be a gap between the existing outside of each furniture arm and the pattern block (Figure 2). Leave it; this will be fixed later.

If there are folds or puckers at the pin line, leave them, but be sure to match up the notches and center creases of the two patterns when you pin them together.

Two-piece Arms with Top Boxing: Place the inside arm patterns over the arms, leaving the 4″ overlap (tuck-ins) on the deck. Pin the top edge of each inside arm pattern to the seam line of the boxing, leaving a 2″ overlap fitting allowance. Secure the bottom edge of each outside arm pattern to the bottom edge or skirtline of the furniture piece with T-pins. You will make a pattern for the top boxing later.

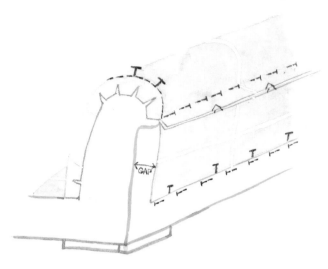

FIGURE 2

pin-fitting a deep scroll

where the inside arms meet the inside back

Smooth the inside back pattern over each arm, clipping until it lies flat. Clip the inside arms if necessary. Pin the two sections together until they fit. If there is a crevice at the junctures of each arm and the back, feel with your hand where it begins and ends. Clip the fitting allowances and pin the arm and back pattern blocks to the point where the crevices begin. On the allowances, mark the word "tuck" (Figure 3). This section will be extended 4" when you cut the actual fabric.

If there is no crevice between the inside arm and back, pin the two sections together, clipping the allowances as you shape the pieces over the curves.

FIGURE 3

marking a tuck-in

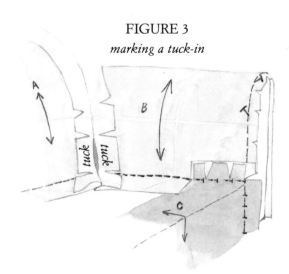

where the outside arms meet the outside back

Smooth the outside back pattern over the outside arms, clipping until the allowances lie flat. Pin the two sections together until they fit (Figure 4).

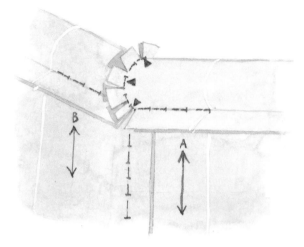

FIGURE 4

fitting the outside arm and back

(C) front

The front section (C) may be constructed in a variety of ways. It can run from inside arm to inside arm, or extend the entire width of the furniture piece. On furniture with T-shaped cushions, the front often extends a few inches around to the side. Keep the front section in one piece wherever possible.

One-piece Front: Cut a pattern block according to the measurements on your scale-size cut-out. Fold it from end to end and steam press the crease. Transfer the directional arrow and letter.

Multi-piece Front: On a long sofa the front may have to be pieced down the middle. On a chaise, the front may have to be pieced in three or four sections.

For a two-piece front, add 1" to the length measurement on your cut-out before cutting the pattern block. Fold the pattern block in half, end to end, and steam press. Cut on the fold. For three pieces, add 1½", and fold the pattern block in thirds. Cut on the folds. For four pieces, add 2" and fold the pattern block end to end twice. Cut the pattern block on the folds. Transfer the directional arrows and the letters to all pieces.

pin-fitting the (C) front

Find the center front on the sofa or chair and mark it with a pin. Place the center crease line of the front pattern piece over the pin to secure. If the section is in two pieces, overlap them at the center by ½″ and pin. Lay the 4″ overlap (tuck-in) onto the deck. Pin the pattern block to the chair at 6″ intervals on either side of the center at the point where the front and deck meet. If you are pinning a long front piece around the curved edge of a chaise, clip the overlap at 3″ intervals so it will lie flat.

If you want the slipcover front to extend around to the side, pin the front around the corner to the point where it meets the outside arms. On the deck there will be a triangular– shaped flap at each corner. Pin this flap on the diagonal, starting from the front corner, until the section lies smoothly on the deck (Figure 5). Trim, leaving a ½″ fitting allowance.

where the front meets the arms

Pin the two sections together, clipping until the two sections lie flat.

arm fronts

Extended Arm Fronts: For arms that extend from the front of the chair to the back, measure the length and width of the front and top panel and add 4″ to both dimensions. Cut two pattern pieces to these dimensions.

Place the panels over each arm and begin pinning at the bottom of the arm fronts. Pin each arm front to the ends of the front piece and to the edges of the inside and outside arm (Figure 1).

Pin the remaining edge of each arm front to the inside back in the same way you pinned the inside arm to the inside back, clipping around the curves so they lie flat.

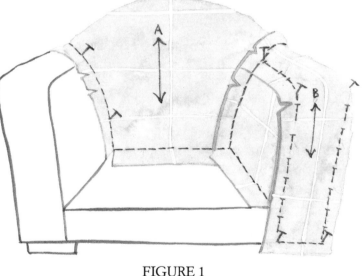

FIGURE 1
pin-fitting extended arm fronts

Separate Arm Fronts: Cut a small piece of sheet or muslin and place it over the front of each arm. Pencil in the outline. Measure 2″ out from the pencil line and cut out two patterns.

Pin the patterns to the inside and outside arms. Clip the inside and outside arm patterns in order to

FIGURE 5
pin-fitting an extended front

pin them smoothly to the arm fronts, but don't clip the arm fronts.

Deep Scroll Arm Fronts: Cut a small piece of sheet or muslin and place it over the front of each arm, tracing the arm front pattern to accommodate the gap between the existing outside arm and the altered one you are creating for a slipcover.

Pencil in the outline. Measure 2″ out from the pencil line on all sides and cut out two patterns. On the slipcover, these sections will be interfaced for additional body so the gap will not be detected.

Pin the arm front patterns to the inside and outside patterns. Clip the inside and outside arm patterns in order to pin them smoothly, but do not clip the arm fronts (Figure 2).

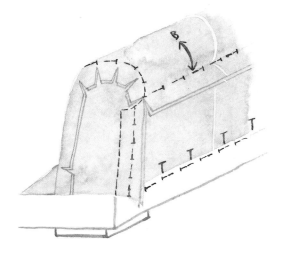

FIGURE 2
pin-fitting deep-scroll arm fronts

shoulders and boxing

Look over your piece of furniture for any areas still not covered. There is likely to be a shoulder area between the inside and outside back or boxing on top of the arms or back. Cut a small piece of sheet or muslin and place it over each area. Pencil in the outline. Measure 2″ out from the pencil line on all sides and cut out the patterns. Pin-fit in place. If any small patterns are on an angle, mark them with a vertical arrow to indicate the straight grain. Leave any puckers or excess fabric alone for now.

wings

Cut the patterns as for the shoulders and boxing, cutting a piece for the inside and outside of each wing. Pin the inner edges of the wing pattern fronts to the inside back (Figure 3). Pin the outer edges of the wing pattern backs to the outer wing backs of the furniture piece.

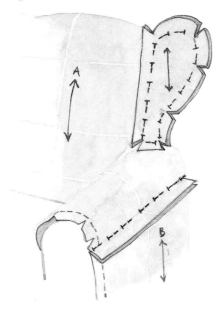

FIGURE 3
pin-fitting wings

where three sections meet

These junctions are not as difficult to work with as you might think, but they must be well marked. It is also necessary to clip one or more of the sections so that all three seams can be pinned together (Figure 4).

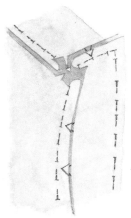

FIGURE 4

finishing up

All the sections are now joined, except the deck, which you don't need a pattern for. You will now pay attention to the areas where the patterns bunch up, creating puckers and folds. These are probably the same areas where the existing upholstery is also gathered, tucked with darts, or eased. Unless you have stylistic differences with the way the upholstery is constructed, follow the original.

Where two sections meet at a curve, mark both with numbered lines. Do the same careful marking where three sections meet.

making darts

If there are darts on the existing upholstery, you should duplicate their placement. Many small darts will lie more smoothly around a curve than a few large ones. Pinch and pin the pattern around the curves and draw a pencil line between the pin marks. Mark each dart from the narrowest point to the widest point (Figure 5).

Try to line up darts on adjoining patterns whenever possible. There will be more fabric to tuck into darts on the inside of a curve than on the outside.

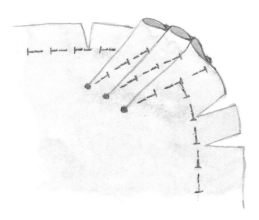

FIGURE 5

gathering and easing

If you prefer the smoother contours that gathering produces, mark where the bunched up area begins and ends (Figure 6). You will gather or ease these areas with pins when you are stitching the slipcover.

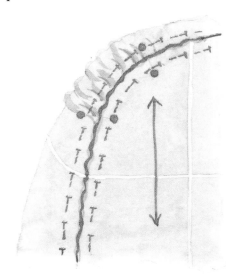

FIGURE 6
easing a curve

basting

Now the patterns are pinned together over the whole piece of furniture, and you can hand baste the entire slipcover together at the pin lines; use brightly colored thread. Remove the pins as you baste, leaving the areas for darts and gathers pinned but unstitched. You may find when you have finished basting that some areas need to be adjusted. Re-baste, or draw a red pencil line where the adjusted seam should go. Mark the arm pieces "right" and "left."

With a pencil, mark the seam line between the basting stitches, using letters or other codes to match up patterns. These will be transferred to the slipcover fabric, so make whatever marks you think will help you match sections and stitch accurately.

Tuck in the overlaps all around the deck. Sit in the furniture piece carefully and check the tuck-ins. If there is too much tension on the inside back and arms, or the tuck-ins are coming loose, you will need to deepen them. Mark the areas to be lengthened "More Tuck." When you lay out the patterns you will allow for an additional 2″–4″, to make a deeper tuck-in.

do you need a closure?

Carefully pull off the sewn-together patterns. If they are too tight to remove, the slipcover will need a closure. This might be a zipper in the back or side, or under an arm, a Velcro™ strip, buttons, or ties—depending on what you want.

Remove the basting stitches where the closure will be, making sure the opening is large enough to enable the cover to slip off. Mark the two sections where the closure will be made. Measure and round up to the nearest standard size in inches for a zipper.

final steps

1. Double-check to make sure each section is completely labeled.

2. Clip the basting stitches and remove all the pattern pieces.

3. With a pencil and ruler, straighten the seam lines. Go over any markings that were hard to make when the pattern was draped over the furniture piece.

4. Trim all sides of each pattern block ½″ from the seam line you have drawn.

5. Refold the pattern pieces and steam press the grids back in.

6. If you are scrimping, or have yet to buy your fabric, take the final measurements of each cloth pattern piece. To do this, measure the length and width at the widest points. Re-cut your ¼″ scale cut-outs to these new dimensions, also cutting any places where the patterns have been cut. Return to the layout strips on pages 74–75 and see if the cutouts can be laid out differently. It may be possible to save a considerable yardage at this point.

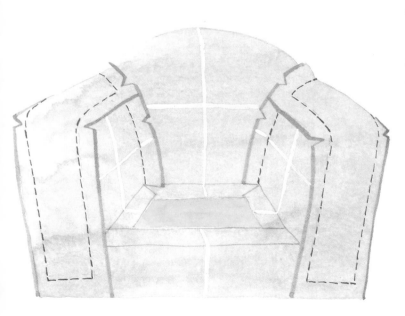

basting the pattern pieces for fit

pillow covers

Slipcovering a pillow is one of the easiest of all sewing tasks. It is also especially good for trying out a yard or two of fabric you might be considering for a bigger project, such as a sofa or chair slipcover. That way, the fabric can not only be put to a visual test, but also to the the test of washing and steam pressing, before a major purchase is made. This will prevent unhappy outcomes with material that may look beautiful on the bolt, but that turns out to be difficult to launder or hard to handle when sewing.

Importantly, making your own pillow covers also offers the opportunity for creating individual designs and working with superior fabrics and trims. Moreover, you are likely to end up with a pillow that looks much better, and costs far less, than any you could purchase.

Pure cottons, linens, damasks, silks, silk blends, or any other light or medium weight fabrics of good quality and fine weave are recommended for most pillows. Vintage linens, worn to a soft patina after years of washing, are particularly desirable, as are pieces of heirloom lace and needlework, which can be used for a pillow top, or for decorative appliqué. Some covers can also be stitched from heavyweight tapestry and drapery fabrics.

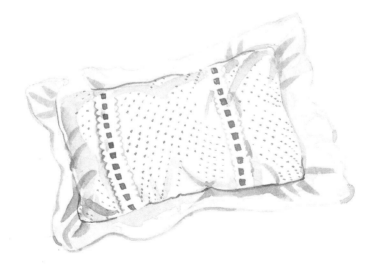

about pillow forms

You can make a slipcover to give new life to an old pillow you already own, or to cover a commercially made pillow form. Pillow forms come in three basic shapes (round, square, and rectangular) and in a range of sizes. Standard sizes generally start at 12″ (measured seam to seam) for accent pillows and run up to 34″ or more for European squares and floor pillows. Bed pillows come in three basic sizes: Standard (20″ × 27″), Queen (20″ × 30″), and King (20″ × 37″).

The best pillow forms are those made of down or a combination of down and feathers. Most com-

mercial forms, however, are made of polyester foam or Dacron fiberfill. For a softer look, these pillow forms can be wrapped in polyester or cotton batting. Their advantage is that they can go right into the washing machine and dryer with or without their covers.

preparations

The instructions in this chapter are for covering simple pillows with only two sides—front and back. Rectangular and square pillows made this way are known as "knife-edged.") Cushions with sides are called "box" cushions (see Chapter Five, pages 117–118).

All of the pillow covers can be stitched by hand or made on a machine with minimal sewing skills. They are especially recommended for beginners who may not be ready to tackle the more difficult aspects of slipcover making that involve working with box cushions or irregular shapes.

The six projects are presented in order of difficulty, ranging from a simple rectangular sham to a majestic Turkish pillow cover. Each presents a new lesson and the opportunity to develop a skill needed to make a more complicated slipcover.

All of the instructions can be adapted to any pillow size. A yard of fabric measuring 48″ or wider should be enough to cover most pillows, but additional fabric is necessary for self–welting and for large-size bed pillows, Turkish pillows, and medallion pillows. (See individual projects for details.)

boudoir pillow sham

A boudoir sham is the bed pillow's daytime dress, slipped directly over the pillow (and pillow case) when the bed is made. It can also be used for small accent pillows. This is the easiest type of pillow cover to make, because it requires no closure. Purely decorative, such a sham is often edged with a ruffle or other romantic looking trim, and offers an ideal place to show off a piece of antique lace.

Any fabric that can be easily washed and is soft to the touch is appropriate for a boudoir sham.

Pieces cut from the corners of vintage damask table-cloths are excellent for this purpose, as they often remain in good condition even if the top of the cloth is stained. Silk or silk satin is another good choice, but need to be hand stitched because they are slippery. One yard of fabric measuring at least 48″ wide will yield one standard bed pillow sham; add ½ yard for Queen and King bed pillow sizes.

1. Prepare the fabric following the instructions in Chapter Three, pages 77–78.

2. With a cloth tape, measure the pillow from seam to seam and cut a paper pattern to these dimensions. (You can also use an existing pillow case as a pattern; be sure to steam press it flat before beginning to work.)

3. Trim the fabric piece so that the corners are square and the grain is straight. Lay the fabric flat, with the right side up, and place the pattern in the top left corner flush with the left selvage (Figure 1). Pin.

4. Mark a line on the fabric 1″ from the edge of the pattern on two sides, as shown. This provides a ½″ seam allowance on all four sides. Cut along the marked line. Remove the pins and pattern, and steam press. This will be the sham front.

5. Use the sham front as a pattern for the sham back, placing it wrong side up on the fabric piece in the bottom right corner. Pin. Mark a line 7″ to the left of the sham front, creating a back 7″ wider. The extra fabric is needed to create the overlap in the back of the sham. Cut out the sham back, following along the pattern side and the new extended lines. Remove the pins.

6. Fold the sham back in half with the right sides together, left to right, so that the crease runs vertically and corners 1 and 2 line up (Figure 2). Steam press the crease, then open the sham and cut along the crease to make two sham back pieces.

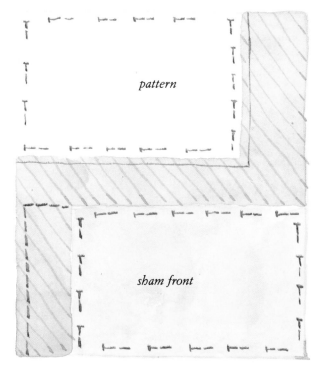

pattern

sham front

FIGURE 1

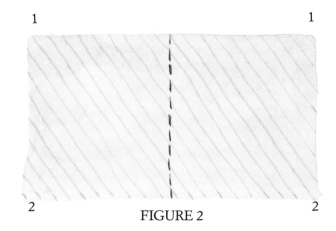

1   1

2   2

FIGURE 2

7. Place the two back sections flat, with the wrong side up. To make a hem for each piece, turn over the edge you have just cut ¼", steam press it flat, and topstitch. Measure 4" in from hemmed edge A and mark line B (Figure 3). Fold edge A over to meet line B, and steam press at the fold. Topstitch down edge A again, directly over the first line of stitches. Do the same with the other back sham section.

8. Lay the two sham back sections wrong side up and place the hemmed edge of the

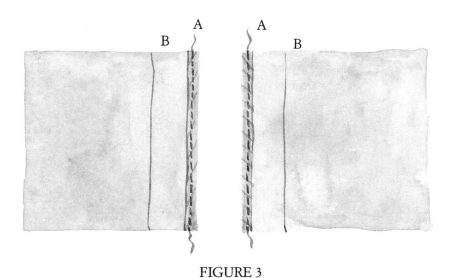

FIGURE 3

FIGURE 4
overlapping back pieces

right section over the hemmed edge of the left section, creating a 2½″ overlap. Baste along the seam line at either end of the overlap to secure (Figure 4). The sham back is now one piece, the same size as the sham front. If you are stitching an appliqué to your sham, stitch it in place on the right side of the pillow front now. (See Chapter Six, pages 121–122.)

9. Place the sham back on top of the sham front, with the right sides together, and pin at each corner. Then pin every few inches along the seam line, keeping the raw edges aligned. Stitch a ½″ seam on all four sides. Remove the pins, clip the corners and and trim the seams to ¼″. Steam press the seams open.

10. Turn the sham right side out. Steam press the entire pillow sham, then topstitch ¼″ in from the edge on all four sides. Steam press again.

flanged throw

A simple pillow cover with a flange, or tailored hem, is often used for a chair cushion, as it can be secured with ties attached out of sight under the hem. A flanged pillow also makes an elegant throw.

This style is well suited to stripes, florals, and small overall patterns, and is a good choice for designs with center motifs, as well as for polished chintzes and lush velveteens. You can also appliqué a square of embroidery or needlepoint, or a piece of vintage lace or chintz; the flange border will become an effective frame.

1. Prepare the fabric following the instructions in Chapter Three, pages 77–78.

2. With a cloth tape, measure the pillow from seam to seam. Add 3½″ on all sides and cut a paper pattern to these dimensions.

3. Using this pattern, follow the instructions for the Boudoir Pillow Sham, Steps 3–9, page 91.

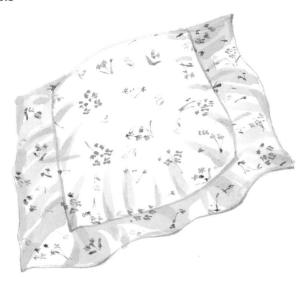

4. When the sham is completed, steam press it flat. Mark a light pencil line 2″ in from each edge to make an inner square. Hand baste through both layers of fabric over this line with the same thread you will use for the final topstitching. (Without hand basting, the material will slide and pucker.) Carefully topstitch directly over the basting stitches (there is no need to remove them). Steam press the finished sham.

topstitching

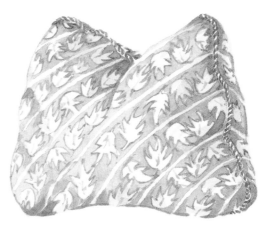

bias square with self-welting

A pillow cover cut on the bias—diagonally to the fabric grain—has a wonderful floppiness to it, but sewing a seam that is cut on the bias can be a trial. The easiest way to keep fabric from slipping out of line is to use one with a striped pattern. This gives you a guide to follow as you pin, cut, and stitch. Fabrics such as duck and faille, which have a diagonal rib to their weave, are particularly pleasing when cut on the bias.

The back of the cover has a facing that can be closed with hand stitching; avoid zippers and

Velcro™ as neither has the necessary give for the floppy pillow shape. A down or feather form is recommended.

1. Prepare the fabric following the instructions in Chapter Three, pages 77–78.

2. With a cloth tape, measure the pillow from seam to seam. Add ½″ on all four sides for the seam allowance and cut a paper pattern to these dimensions.

3. Trim the fabric piece so that the corners are square and the grain is straight. Lay the fabric flat, right side up, with the selvages to the left and right. Line up the pattern piece, with points A and D touching the top and left edges. To make the pillow front, pin the pattern in place and cut out along the edges. Remove the pins and pattern.

4. Lay out the remainder of the fabric wrong side up. Using the pillow front as a pattern for the pillow back, place it right side up on the fabric in the top left corner (Figure 2). Pin. Measure out 2″ as shown, extending the line between points B and C to points E and F, and mark.

5. Cut out the pillow back along the pattern edge, then cut along the extended line to make a 2″ strip for the closure facing.

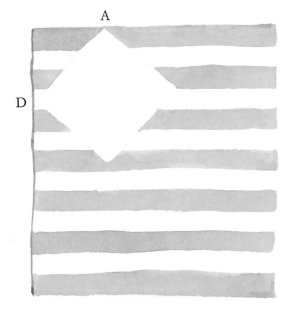

FIGURE 1

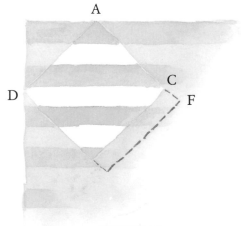

FIGURE 2

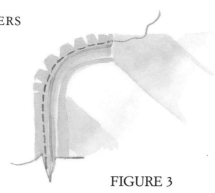

6. For instructions on how to prepare welting, see Chapter Six, pages 139–141. Lay the pillow top right side up. Starting 3″ from one corner, align the raw edges of the welting casing with the raw edge of the pillow top. Pin in place and clip the corners (Figure 3). This allows the welting to gently curve around the corners. Trim the welting, leaving a 2″ tail.

FIGURE 3

7. Stitch, sewing directly over the welting casing seam, moving the wheel of the machine by hand around the corners. Turn the pillow top wrong side up, so that the welting is on the wrong side, and clip the corners. (For instructions on finishing the welting, see Chapter Six, page 141.)

FIGURE 4

8. Lay the closure facing piece wrong side up and fold up a ¼″ hem (Figure 4). Steam press flat and topstitch.

9. Lay the closure facing strip on the pillow back, with the right sides together, aligning the raw edges and stripes (Figure 5). Stitch a ½″ seam.

10. Open the two pieces and turn them wrong side up. Steam press them flat, pressing the seam down toward the pillow back. With the wrong sides together, fold the facing down toward the pillow back and steam press. Topstitch the facing to the pillow back directly over the existing hem stitching.

FIGURE 5

11. Place the pillow front and back with the right sides together and the closure facing at top. With the pillow front toward you, pin together on all four sides. Stitch a ½″ seam along the existing welting seam line around all sides except the faced closure (Figure 6). Here, stitch only 1″ beyond the corners at points A and B. Remove the pins. Clip the curves and trim the seams, taking care not to cut into the closure facing.

12. Turn the pillow case inside out and slip it over the pillow form. Align the facing edge with the welting seam line and pin. Slipstitch.

FIGURE 6

ruffled pillow round

This simple round pillow cover with a sham closure is dressed up with a heavy ruffle that camouflages the slight pucker produced by the curved seam. Because the ruffle adds an extra layer to sew through, a soft, lightweight fabric is suggested. Solid colors or small prints are recommended; ½ yard of matching fabric is needed for the two-sided ruffle.

1. Prepare the fabric following the instructions in Chapter Three, pages 77–78.

2. Measure the diameter of the pillow from seam to seam.

3. To make a pattern, lay a piece of paper flat on a work surface that you can push a pin into. Secure a push pin in the paper; attach a piece of string to the pin and to a sharp pencil, so that the string extends one half the diameter plus ½" for seam allowance. Using the string as a guide, draw a circle with the pencil and cut out along the marked line (Figure 1).

4. Using the pattern, cut two circles from your fabric. Fold one circle in half and steam press the crease. Cut along the crease. You will now have two back pieces.

5. Draw a rectangle on a piece of paper. For the length, use the measurement you have calculated in Step 2 plus 1". The width should be 2". Using this as a pattern, cut two pieces of fabric (Figure 2). These will be your two closure facings.

6. Lay one closure facing piece wrong side up and fold up a ¼" hem as shown (Figure 3). Steam press it flat and topstitch. Repeat for the second closure facing piece.

7. Place one closure facing strip on one pillow back piece, with right sides together, aligning the straight edges. Stitch a ½" seam (Figure 4). Repeat for the second closure facing and back piece.

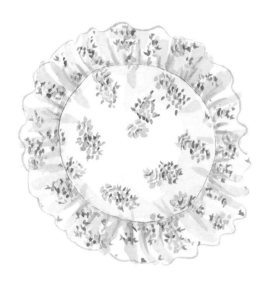

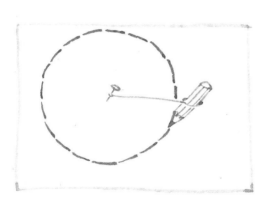

FIGURE 1

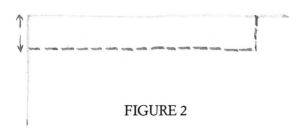

FIGURE 2

8. Open the two pieces and turn them wrong side up. Steam press them flat, pressing the seam down toward the pillow back piece. With the wrong sides together, fold the facing down toward the pillow back piece and steam press again. Top-stitch the facing to the pillow back directly over the existing hem stitching. Trim the bottom corners of the facing to align with the circle curve. Repeat for the second closure facing and back piece.

9. Make a self-faced ruffle 4″ wide following the instructions in Chapter Six, pages 132–133. Seam the ruffle ends to make a circle, and adjust the circle to fit the pillow front.

10. Place the circular ruffle on the pillow front, aligning the raw edges. Leave the ruffles folded in toward the center of the pillow front (Figure 5).

11. Place the two pillow back pieces over the pillow front with the wrong sides up, overlapping the straight edges of the back sections by 1″. Pin the pieces together and baste along the seam line (Figure 6). The ruffle will be sandwiched between the pillow front and back pieces.

12. Stitch the pillow front and back sections together all the way around the circle with a ½″ seam. Remove the pins and basting. Trim the seam to ¼″ and clip at 3″ intervals. Steam press the seam away from the pillow case.

13. Turn the pillow case right side out. Steam press well and topstitch ¼″ from the seam all the way around. Slip the case over your pillow form and secure with slipstitching.

FIGURE 3

FIGURE 4

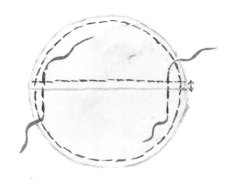

FIGURE 5

FIGURE 6

shirred medallion round

A medallion pillow, in which a fabric motif is framed by the shape of the pillow itself, provides a good place to set off a large-scale floral motif, and looks especially effective when used on a piece of furniture slipcovered in the same material. One large motif works well on the pillow front, while two smaller elements—leaves or smaller flowers, perhaps—are best for the pillow back, which has an overlapped closure in the center.

Recommended fabrics include chintz, toile, vintage drapery fabric, or any good quality cotton or linen with a design motif measuring at least six inches across. Loose hand gathering, or shirring, along the seam line gives the finished piece an elegant pouf.

1. Prepare your fabric following the instructions in Chapter 3, page 10.

2. Lay out your piece of fabric, then choose the floral motif you wish to feature on your pillow front. Calculate the diameter of the circle size you want, making sure to accommodate the floral motif, as well as enough background to set it off. Add 1″ for the seam allowance. Buy or make a pillow round to fit the dimensions your circle requires.

3. Following Step 3 for the Ruffled Pillow Round on page 12, cut a tracing paper pattern to your dimensions. Place the pattern over the fabric and adjust it until the floral motif falls within the circle in the way that you want. Pin the pattern in place and cut one fabric piece for the pillow front.

4. Remove the pins and fold your paper pattern in half; cut it in two along the crease. Place the pattern on your fabric over the design motifs you have chosen for the pillow back; pin, and cut. Remove the pins.

5. Following Steps 5–8 for the Ruffled Pillow Round on page 12, cut the closure facings and stitch them to the back pieces. (Do not make a ruffle.)

6. Place the two pillow back pieces over the pillow front with the right sides together, overlapping the straight edges 1″. Pin together and baste along the seam line.

7. Using a ½″ seam, stitch the pillow front and back together all the way around the circle. Remove the pins. Trim the seam to ¼″ and clip at 3″ intervals. Steam press the seam open.

8. With the pillow case wrong side out, loosely shirr the pillow seam, following the directions in Chapter 7, page 98. Turn the pillow case right side out and press. Cover the seam line with trim, such as braid or cording. Slip the case over your pillow form and secure the closure with slipstitching.

turkish pillow

This luxurious pillow cover appears three-dimensional but is actually made out of only two pieces of fabric. You can use a knife-edged pillow form, or a box cushion form, which won't look like a box once it is stuffed inside the finished pillow case. The total effect depends on the trim: tassels and rich braid mask the single seam.

Recommended fabrics for this pillow include velvets, and heavy woven and drapery-weight yardage. The pillow top can also be made from vintage drapery fabric, a small hooked rug, or a bit of lightweight carpet. Making the bottom piece from a lighter fabric, such as felt, duck or velveteen, will reduce the bulk when the top and bottom are joined.

1. Prepare your fabric following the instructions in Chapter 3, page 76.

2. Measure your pillow form from seam to seam (a minimum of 20″ is recommended.) Add ½″ on all sides and cut two fabric pieces to these dimensions. (If you are using a box cushion form, don't forget to include the sides in your measurements. For instance, if your box cushion is 20″ square with 4″ sides, each fabric piece should be 23″ square.) If you wish to pad your cushion following the directions in Chapter 3, page 45, do so at this stage.

3. Place the fabric pieces right sides together. Following the directions in Chapter 7, pages 80–86, insert a Velcro™ fastener or zipper along one edge of the pillow, centering it at least 4″ from both corners.

4. Stitch the remaining three sides of the pillow, right sides together, using a ½″ seam. Referring to Figure 1, with the pillow case still inside out, mark 3″ in from each corner at points A. Mark a diagonal line across the corner of the fabric to join these points. Repeat for each corner. These will be your gathering lines.

5. Referring to Figure 2, gather tightly along the diagonal lines, following the directions for Traditional Machine Gathering in Chapter 7, page 89. The pillow case will now have four "ears."

6. Open the fastener and turn the pillow case right side out, leaving the ears inside; this will produce rounded corners. Close the fastener and apply trim along the seam line. Stitch a generous tassel to each corner.

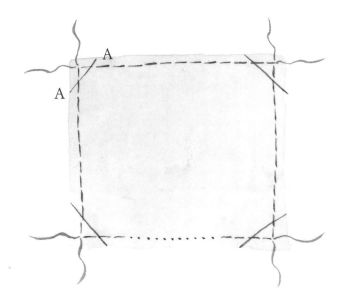

FIGURE 1
each corner is marked

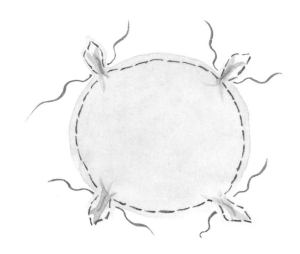

FIGURE 2
gathering produces a rounded shape

sewing a slipcover

The directions in this chapter cover all the basic steps needed for cutting and sewing a slipcover, and can be adapted to any design. They start with armchairs, sofas, and chaises then move on to armless chairs, daybeds, ottomans, and box cushions. If you prepared carefully, the actual sewing should go quickly. With a final fitting, your furniture will be transformed with a beautiful slipcover that should last for years.

cutting the fabric

Before you cut, be sure you have tested the fabric for shrinkage according to the instructions in Chapter Three, page 77. (If your sample has shrunk more than ⅛″ after steam pressing, you will need to account for this when you cut the fabric by adding back the amount of shrinkage to each section.) As you cut, unfold only enough yardage for one slipcover section at a time, and always cut on a single layer of fabric with the right side up following the sequence established on the layout strip.

If you are using a pattern, place the pattern pieces on the fabric with the marked sides up and pin to secure. For a directional fabric pattern, be sure to cut the slipcover sections on the lengthwise grain. (Place the pattern pieces so that the arrows run parallel to the selvages. If not using a pattern, cut each section so its lengthwise edge is parallel to the selvages.)

centering motifs

If the fabric has large-scale motifs, you need to pay attention to how they fall within each slipcover section. In general, dominant motifs look best slightly above center, except on cushions, where they should be centered exactly. When not using a pattern, check the placement by eye. For cloth patterns, use the steam pressed crease lines as a guide, lifting the pattern up to see how it is positioned on the fabric. If you need to match motifs from one section to another, place the pattern pieces on the fabric in exactly the same way for both sections. It will never be possible to match two sections at every point along a seam, but if the major motifs are symmetrical, the overall effect will be pleasing.

marking

It is important to transfer your marks from the pattern to each slipcover section. Unpin the pattern but leave it in place. Slip a sheet of dressmaker's carbon "ink"-side-up under the fabric and run over the seam lines with a tracer's wheel. You can transfer other marks with a #2 pencil, but when marking on the right side of fabric, use a tailor's pencil. Cloth patterns will be notched and clipped from the pin-fitting process. Transfer the notches and clips with a pencil, but do not actually cut them into the fabric when you are cutting out the sections.

sewing

As you sew, pin the sections so that all the notches and marks are matched, and machine baste the seams before final stitching. Unless otherwise indicated, stitch all seams with a ½″ seam, with the right sides of the fabric together. Steam press all seams open as you work. If you are quilting any sections, do so before you begin sewing the slipcover (see Chapter Six, pages 128–131).

welting (see Chapter Six, pages 139–141)

If you are going to use welting, have it assembled and coiled before you start. Welting is always stitched to one slipcover section before that section is seamed to another. For example, you would add the welting to a cushion top before sewing on the boxing (side) strips. Stitch the welting with a zipper foot to the section that has the least gathering or number of darts. If you are welting most seams, use a zipper foot to stitch the entire slipcover.

If you need to cross two welted seams, pull out the first and last ½″ of welting cord sewn to each seam line and trim it off. When the sections are seamed, the welting casing but not the cord will be stitched.

covering an armchair, sofa, or chaise

These furniture pieces require cloth patterns (see Chapter Three, pages 78–86). If the inside back and arm patterns are marked for extended tuck-ins, extend these now to 2″ and mark with a pencil after the pattern is pinned to the fabric (Figure 1).

If you are lining any slipcover sections, cut the lining pieces as you cut the sections. Pin the two together and treat them as one as you sew. (You can also use the patterns as lining.)

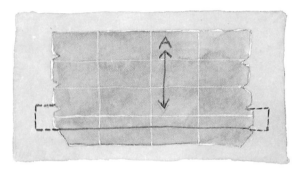

FIGURE 1

cutting a one-piece back with extended tuck-ins

cutting the sections

(A) back

One-piece Back: Pin the pattern and cut out the section, including any extended tuck-ins. Mark.

Two-Piece Back: Be sure to position the pattern crease marks in the same way for both sections if using a fabric with dominant motifs. Pin the patterns and cut out the two sections, including any extended tuck-ins. Mark.

Two-Piece Back with Boxing: Pin the patterns and cut out the inside and outside back sections, including any extended tuck-ins. Cut out the boxing piece. Mark.

One-Piece Back with Center Seam: Be sure to position the pattern crease marks in the same way for both sections if using a fabric pattern with dominant motifs. Pin the patterns and cut out sections A-1 and A-2, including any extended tuck-ins. Mark.

Two-Piece Back with Center Seam: Be sure to position the pattern crease marks in the same way for all four sections if working with a fabric with dominant motifs. Pin the patterns and cut out sections A-1, A-2, A-1 "outside," and A-2 "outside," including any extended tuck-ins. Mark.

Channeled or Barrel Back: Be sure to position the pattern pieces on the fabric in the same way for all the sections. Pin the patterns and cut out each inside back section, including extended tuck-ins; repeat for the outside back section. Mark.

(B) arms

One-Piece Arms: Pin the patterns and cut out one section for each arm, including any extended tuck-ins. Mark.

Two-Piece Arms: Be sure to position the pattern crease marks in the same way for the two sections to be seamed for each arm. Pin the patterns and cut out the two sections for each arm, including any extended tuck-ins. Mark.

Two-Piece Arms with Boxing: Pin the patterns and cut out the two sections for each arm, including any extended tuck-ins. Cut out the two boxing pieces. Mark.

(C) front

One-Piece Front: Pin the patterns and cut out the one section. Mark.

Multi-Piece Front: Be sure to position the pattern crease marks in the same way on all the sections. Pin the patterns and cut out all sections. Mark.

arm fronts

Pin the patterns and cut out one section for each arm. Avoid centering a large motif on the arm fronts. Mark.

shoulders

Pin the patterns and cut out one section for each shoulder. Even if the sections are an odd shape, be sure they are cut on the straight grain. Mark.

wings

Pin the patterns and cut out one section for each wing. Mark. Even if the sections are an odd shape, be sure they are cut on the straight grain. Avoid centering a large motif on the wings.

(D and E) box cushions

See pages 116–118. Cut these so dominant motifs are centered on the top and bottom.

skirt

See pages 112–115.

sewing the sections

Before you stitch a seam, sew any darts, and gather sections according to the marks you have transferred from the pattern pieces. Staystitch along any seam lines where a section is to be eased (see Chapter Six, page 125). Be sure to seam the sections in the proper sequence, starting with the (A) Back.

(A) back

One-Piece Back: This is ready to go.

Two-Piece Back without Boxing: Sew the inside and outside back sections together at the top seam line stitching in the welting if there is any (Figure 2).

Two-Piece Back with Boxing: If there is welting, stitch it to the boxing along both long edges. Sew the inside edge of the boxing section to the top edge of the inside back section at the seam line. Sew the outside edge of the boxing section to the top edge of the outside back section (Figure 3).

One-Piece Back with a Center Seam: Sew sections A-1 and A-2 at the center seam line. Leave an opening in the outside back for the closure, if there is one.

Two-Piece Back with Center Seams: Sew sections A-1 and A-2 together at the center seam line. Repeat for sections A-1 "outside" and A-2 "outside" (Figure 4). Leave an opening in the outside back for the closure, if there is one. Sew the inside and outside back pieces together at the top seam line, stitching in welting, if there is any.

FIGURE 2
Two-piece back without boxing

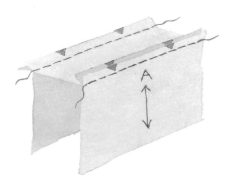

FIGURE 3
Two-piece back with boxing

FIGURE 4
Two-piece back with center seams

Channeled or Barrel Back: Staystitch along the seam lines of each front section. Sew along the edge of the center channel to the edge of the adjoining channel. If the edges are deeply curved, clip the seam allowances. Repeat for the remaining edge of the center channel and the adjoining channel. Repeat for any remaining channels (Figure 5). Sew the pieced inside back to the outside back along the top seam line, stitching in the welting if there is any.

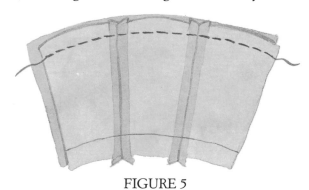

FIGURE 5
Channeled back

(B) arms
One-Piece Arms: These are ready to go.

Two-Piece Arms: Sew the inside and outside back sections together at the top seam line, stitching in welting if there is any.

Two-Piece Arms with Top Boxing: Sew the inside edge of the boxing section to the top edge of each inside arm section at the seam line, stitching in welting if there is any. Sew the outside edge of the boxing section to the top edge of each outside arm section, stitching in welting if there is any.

Two-Piece Arms with Extended Boxing: Sew the inside edge of the extended boxing strip to the front and top edges of each inside arm section at the seam line, stitching in welting if there is any. Sew the outside edge of the extended boxing strip to the front and top edges of the outside arm section, stitching in welting if there is any.

sewing the inside arms to the back

If there is welting, stitch it from the bottom edge of the outside back to the top of the tuck-in on the inside back on each side.

Machine baste the inside arms and boxing, if there is any, to the inside back along the seam lines. Clip the seams at frequent intervals so they lie flat. Place the basted sections over the furniture piece and adjust the fit. If the sections don't fit, remove the basting and re-baste. When satisfied with the fit, stitch the seams using the normal stitch setting.

sewing the arm fronts to the inside and outside arms

Cut two pieces of interfacing, using the arm front sections as patterns. Trim ½″ all the way around the edges. Baste or fuse the interfacing onto the wrong side of each arm front section. Staystitch on the seam line all around except for the bottom edge (Figure 1).

If there is welting, stitch it around each completed arm front from one bottom edge around to the other. Sew the completed arm sections to the arm fronts with the right sides together and the arm fronts on top. Start at one bottom edge and end at the other (Figure 2). Steam press all seam allowances toward the arm fronts. The bottoms of the arm fronts will hang free; these will be seamed to the (C) front later.

sewing the arms to the (C) front

If the front needs to be seamed in sections, do so now. If the front extends around the sides, sew the darts at each end, clip, and steam press them flat (see Chapter Three, page 83).

With the right sides together, pin the ends of the front to the bottom inside edges of the arm front sections and to the bottom of the inside arms as far as the tuck-ins. Clip the seam allowances so they will lie flat (Figure 3).

Machine baste along the seam lines, remove the pins, and check for fit. Make sure neither the arm front nor the front section is being stretched. Readjust if necessary and stitch. On a furniture piece with a T-shaped cushion, where the front extends around the sides by a few inches, follow the seam lines of the arm sections when fitting the arms and front together.

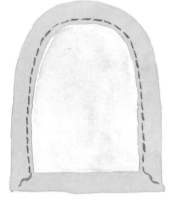

FIGURE 1

putting interfacing on an arm front

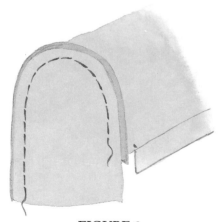

FIGURE 2

sewing on an arm front

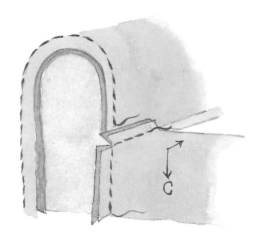

FIGURE 3

sewing an arm front to the (C) front

105

sewing the outside arms to the back

If there are no shoulders, sew the outside arms to the outside back, easing in the darts and gathers.

shoulders

Prepare the shoulder interfacing in the same way as for the arm fronts. Sew the front edge of each shoulder to the inside back. Sew the back edge of each shoulder to the outside back. Sew the bottom edge of each shoulder to the outside arm. Clip the seams well and steam press the seam allowances toward the shoulders. If there is no top boxing, stitch all the way around the shoulder (Figure 1).

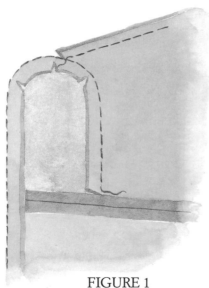

FIGURE 1

sewing a shoulder

wings

Prepare the wing interfacing in the same way as the arm fronts. For each wing, pin one inside and one outside section together and stitch along the curved seam line. Add welting if there is any (Figure 2). Remove the pins. Trim and clip the seams and turn the wings right side out.

Sew the front unstitched edge of each wing to the inside back, and the back unstitched edge of each wing to the outside back, matching the seam lines. Clip the seams and steam press all the seam allowances toward the wings.

FIGURE 2

sewing a wing

deck

Measure the deck, from the edge of the front overlap to the inside back, and from inside arm to inside arm. Add 4″ to each dimension and cut a piece of muslin to these measurements. This will be the deck. Sew the front overlap to one long side of the muslin deck. Steam press the seam allowance toward the deck. Turn under ¼″ on the sides and back of the deck and topstitch (Figure 3). Turn under the raw edges of the tuck-ins ¼″ on the inside arms and back section, steam press, and topstitch. The three sides of the deck are tucked in when the cover is finally fitted. They are not stitched to the rest of the slipcover, so the deck essentially remains an open flap.

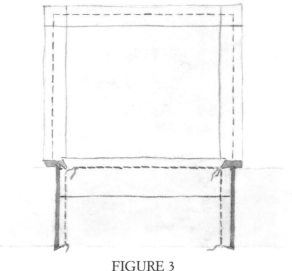

FIGURE 3

sewing the deck

first fitting and closure

When you have stitched all the sections except the skirt, place the cover over the furniture piece and check it carefully for fit. Adjust if necessary, then install any closures (see Chapter Six) before adding the skirt.

If you are using ties, buttons, or Velcro™ for a closure, the open edges of the seams need to be faced. Measure the length of the opening and add 1″. Cut two facing strips to that measurement and 4″ wide. Turn each strip under ¼″ on each end and long side, and steam press. Turn under another ¼″ and steam press again. Topstitch.

Place one facing on one closure edge, with the right sides together, aligning the raw edges. Stitch a ½″ seam. Repeat for the second facing and closure edge. The edges are now ready for a closure.

covering a sofa bed

Most standard sofa beds can be slipcovered following the basic directions for an armchair, sofa, or chaise. To open a sofa bed with the slipcover on, simply untuck the tuck-ins, fold back the deck, and pop the bed through.

finishing a skirtless slipcover

If there is welting, sew it along the bottom. Measure the distance between the legs and add ½″ to each dimension. For each side, cut a piece of fabric as long as this measurement and 3″ wide. These will be the tacking panels.

Turn the short ends and one long side of each tacking panel under ¼″ and topstitch. Remove the slipcover and mark on the wrong side where each panel will begin and end. Place the tacking panels on the marks and stitch with ½″ seams. Put the slipcover on the furniture piece. Turn the tacking panels toward the inside bottom of the furniture piece and secure them with slipstitching, or tack with small nails or staples.

For a slipcover that falls all the way to the floor, turn under the skirt bottom ¼″ and steam press. Turn under another ¼″ and hemstitch.

making tacking panels

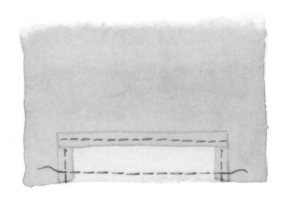

making a skirt

See pages 112–115.

covering box cushions

See pages 116–118.

applying trim

See Chapter Six, pages 137–138.

covering a slipper chair

A slipper chair is an armless chair with a skirt that falls from the seat to the floor. It does not require a cloth pattern (a paper pattern is used).

slipper chair with an attached seat cushion

Before sewing, machine baste all the sections and then slip the cover on. If you can get it on and off, you don't need a closure. If you can't, you need to take out a back side seam and add a zipper or other closure (see Chapter Six).

Back: Measure the inside back from the top of the seat to the the top of the chair, and from side seam to side seam. Add 1″ to each dimension. Cut a piece of fabric to these dimensions. (If the top of the back is curved, trace the outline onto a piece of paper. Add ½″ around the edges, cut out along the line, and use this as a pattern.) Repeat for the outside back, measuring up from the skirtline.

Back Boxing: Measure the length of the boxing from skirtline to skirtline. Add 1″. Measure the width of the boxing from front to back and add 1″. Cut one long strip of boxing to these dimensions.

Seat: Measure from the front skirtline to the inside chair back, and from side skirtline to side skirtline. Add 1″ to each dimension. Cut a piece of fabric to these measurements.

Skirt: See pages 112–115. Measure the height from the floor to the seat bottom and add 2″.

Shaping the Seat: Place the seat section over the seat with the wrong side up. Pin the extra fabric along the two front corners. Remove the fabric section and stitch each pinned front corner to make a dart (Figure 1). Cut the darts open on the diagonal fold lines and steam press them flat.

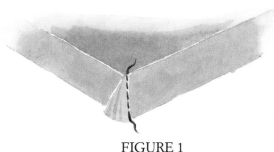

FIGURE 1
shaping the seat

Attaching the Boxing Strip to the Back Sections: If there is welting, stitch it to the boxing strip along both long edges. Sew the back edge of the boxing strip to the top and two sides of the outside back. Sew the inside edge of the boxing strip to the top and two sides of the inside back, centering it and leaving the bottom inside edges free to attach to the seat sides (Figure 2).

FIGURE 2
attaching the boxing

Attaching the Seat: If there is welting, stitch it around the bottom of the seat, boxing strip ends, and outside back. Sew the inside back edge of the seat to the bottom inside edges of the boxing strip and to the bottom of the inside back. Clip at the corners where the boxing, inside back, and seat back come together.

Attaching the Skirt: Sew the top edge of the skirt to the bottom edge of the seat, the bottom edges of the boxing strips and the bottom edge of the outside back. Steam press the seam allowances toward the skirt.

Add 1″ to each dimension. Cut a fabric section according to these measurements.

Skirt: See pages 112–115).

Attaching the Boxing Strip to the Back Sections: If there is welting, stitch it to the boxing strip along both long edges. Sew the back edge of the boxing strip to the top and two sides of the outside back. Sew the inside edge of the boxing strip to the top and two sides of the inside back.

Attaching the Deck: Sew the inside back edge of the deck to the bottom of the inside back. Clip at the corners.

FIGURE 3
attaching the skirt

slipper chair with a separate cushion

Back: Remove the cushion. Measure and cut as for the Slipper Chair with an Attached Seat Cushion, measuring from the deck instead of the seat.

Back Boxing: Measure and cut as for the Slipper Chair with an Attached Seat Cushion.

Deck: Measure from the front skirtline to the inside chair back, and from side skirtline to side skirtline.

Attaching the Skirt: Sew the top edge of the skirt to the three free edges of the deck, the bottom edge of the boxing strips, and the bottom edge of the outside back, stitching in welting if there is any (Figure 3). Steam press the seam allowances toward the skirt.

Covering the Seat Cushion: See Box Cushions, pages 116–118.

Sewing the Back and Seat: Sew the inside back to the outside back, leaving the bottom open. Clip, notching any curves, and trim the seam. Sew the seat back to the bottom of the inside back.

Skirt: Sew the sides to the front and back to make one continuous skirt of four panels.

Attaching the Skirt: Sew the top edge of the skirt to the bottom of the outside back and to the sides and front of the seat, placing a skirt seamline at each corner. Turn under the skirt bottom ¼″ and steam press. Turn under another ¼″ and hemstitch.

draped chair cover

This unwelted slipcover fits loosely over a side or dining chair, gently following its contours. You will need to make a paper pattern for the back. If you are using tissue-thin fabric, make flat-felled seams (see Chapter Six, page 126).

Back: Place a piece of paper over the chair back and trace the outline. Draw a line 1½″ out from the sides and top and 1″ from the bottom. Cut out the pattern on the line. Cut one piece of fabric to the pattern measurements.

Seat: Measure the seat top from front to back and side to side. Add 2″ to each dimension and cut out a piece of fabric to these measurements.

Skirt: Measure the chair height from the floor to the seat top and add 1″. Measure the width of each chair side from outside leg to outside leg and add 1″ to each dimension. Cut two pieces of fabric to these dimensions and the chair height plus 1″. Measure the chair front and back from outside leg to outside leg and add 1″. Cut two pieces of fabric to these dimensions and the chair height plus 1″.

daybed

Most daybeds consist simply of a large covered box cushion, often with a skirted cover that falls from underneath the cushion to the floor.

Deck: Measure from side skirtline to side skirtline and from end skirtline to end skirtline, and add 1″ to each dimension. Cut one fabric section to these dimensions. If the deck area is large, you may have to cut two pieces and seam them down the middle.

Skirt: Measure the height from floor to deck and add 2″. (See pages 112–115.)

Cushions and Bolsters: See Box Cushions, pages 116–118, and Bolsters, page 118.

Attaching the Skirt to the Deck: If there is welting, stitch it all the way around the deck. Sew the top edge of the skirt to the four sides of the deck. Notch the corners and steam press the seam allowances toward the skirt.

ottomans

If your ottoman has a cushion, follow the instructions for box cushions on pages 116–118.

round ottoman

Top: Measure the diameter from seam to seam and add 1″. Make a paper pattern following the directions in Step 3 for Ruffled Pillow Round, Chapter Four, page 96. Cut one fabric section to this measurement.

Boxing: Measure the circumference of the ottoman and add 2″. Divide this number in half. Determine the boxing height you want and add 1½″. Cut two boxing sections to these measurements.

Attaching the Top and Boxing: If there is welting, stitch it all the way around the top section. Sew the ends of the two boxing sections to make a continuous round. Sew one edge of the boxing to the top.

Skirt: Make a gathered skirt according to instructions on page 112. Measure from the floor to the ottoman top. Subtract the height of the boxing and add 2″. If there is no boxing, measure the height from floor to top and add 2″. Measure the circumference and double it. (Triple it for a fuller gather.) Piece the skirt in sections if necessary. Sew the top edge of the skirt to the bottom edge of the boxing. If there is no boxing, sew the skirt directly to the top. Clip the curves and trim the seams.

square or rectangular ottoman with boxing

Top: Measure the top from side to side and end to end, and add 1″ to each dimension. Cut one fabric section to these measurements. Fold it in half twice and steam press the creases.

Boxing: Determine the boxing height you want. Measure the top from side to side and add 1″. Cut two boxing sections to this dimension and the boxing height. Measure the ottoman top from end to end. Cut two boxing sections to this dimension and the boxing height. Fold each strip in half end to end and steam press the crease.

Attaching the Top and Boxing: If there is welting, stitch it to the top section. Sew the boxing strips end to end into a continuous round. Slip the boxing over the ottoman with the wrong side out. Place the top section on the ottoman with the wrong side up and align the creases. Pin the top to the boxing at the seam lines. Remove the pinned sections, and sew the boxing to the top, removing the pins as you go.

Skirt: Make a pleated or gathered skirt following the directions on pages 112–115. Sew the top edge of the skirt to the bottom edge of the boxing.

making a skirt

When using a directional fabric pattern, gathered and box-pleated skirts must be pieced from several sections because these can only be as long as the fabric is wide (see Chapter Three, page 69). The sections are pieced to make one long continuous round that is shortened to the desired size by gathers or pleats. The recommended ratio for a fully gathered skirt is three times the (P) perimeter of the skirtline. A 2-to-1 ratio will yield a less full gather—the choice depends on the look you want. To determine how many sections you need, measure the skirtline all the way around and multiply that number by three (or two). Then divide that number by the width of the fabric.

A tailored skirt with corner kick pleats is made in four sections—one for each side—so that the seams are located at the corners and hidden by the pleats. If the sides of your furniture piece are long, as on a daybed or three-seat sofa, you may have to piece the long sides. Center the extra seams, and make sure you still have one at each corner.

gathered skirt

1. Measure all the way around the skirtline and multiply by three (or two). Measure the height from the floor to the skirtline and add 2″.

2. Make the skirt following the directions for the Lined Ruffle in Chapter Six, page 132. With the right sides together, pin the skirt to the skirtline. If there is a closure in the body of the slipcover, align one of the skirt seam lines with it.

3. Before stitching, snip open the skirt seam at the closure. On one side of the seam, fold the seam allowance of the lining and skirt fabric inward so they are between the lining and fabric sections. Steam press and slipstitch (Figure 1). Repeat on the other side of the seam.

4. Stitch the skirt to the slipcover body at the skirtline with a ½″ seam. Steam press the seam allowances toward the skirt.

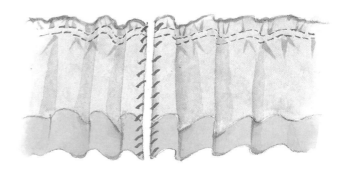

FIGURE 1

tailored skirt with corner kick pleats

This skirt has 3″ deep pleats that meet on a fold line over a seam at each corner.

1. If there is welting, stitch it to the body of the slipcover at the skirtline before you attach the skirt. Slip the cover over the furniture piece with the right side out and secure the skirtline with T-pins so it won't ride up.

2. Measure the sides, front, and back of the furniture piece from corner to corner at the skirtline. Add 13″ to each of the four dimensions. If you are matching pattern motifs, add the inch measurement required by each repeat (see Chapter Three, page 69). Measure from the floor to the skirtline and add 2″.

3. Cut four strips of skirting to these measurements. If you are matching pattern motifs, pin the strips to the furniture piece at the skirtline and align the center of each strip until the motifs on the furniture piece and the skirt match. Trim off the excess at each end.

4. Cut four sections of lining to the same length as the skirting but 1″ shorter in height. Sew each lining piece to each skirt piece following the instructions for the Lined Ruffle in Chapter Six, page 132. Do not stitch the top edges together.

5. Lay each section open, with the lining and fabric wrong side up. Sew each section to the next, end to end with the right sides together, to make one continuous round (Figure 1). Fold the lining and skirt sections right sides out and align the raw edges. Machine baste ½″ from the edges.

FIGURE 1

6. Place the skirt with the lining side up. At the raw edges, mark pleat lines A and B at 3″ intervals on either side of each seam line (Figure 2). At each pleat, pinch the two A marks and bring their folds together over the seam on the right side of the fabric. Crease the fold at lines B to finish the pleats and pin to secure (Figure 3).

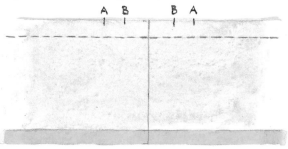

FIGURE 2

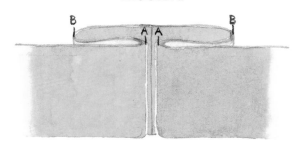

FIGURE 3

7. With the right side out, slip the skirt over the furniture piece and adjust to make sure a pleat is located at each corner. Pin to secure. If there is too much or too little skirt, adjust the pleats to fit.

8. At each corner, readjust the pleat folds to hide the seams. To do so, unpin and fold at lines A and B and move line A around the corner 1″ so the seam can't be seen (Figure 4). Readjust the

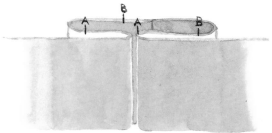

FIGURE 4

pleat and repin. If the slipcover has a closure in a corner seam, do not readjust the corner pleat that falls directly underneath it.

9. Unpin and remove the skirt, repinning each pleat as you go. Steam press each pleat flat.

10. Remove the slipcover. If there is a corner closure, snip open the pleat seam beneath it. Finish following Step 3 for the Gathered Skirt, page 112 (Figure 5). Repin the pleat before sewing on the skirt. Stitch the skirt to the slipcover body at the skirtline with a ½" seam (Figure 6). Steam press the seam allowances toward the skirt.

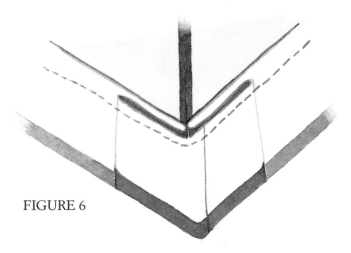

FIGURE 6

tailored skirt with center and corner kick pleats

The skirts for long sofas often have a box pleat at the center front, and two half pleats that meet at the center back below the closure.

1. Measure the front and back of the furniture piece from corner to corner at the skirtline. Add 25" to each dimension. Add 1" to the back measurement. Measure the two short sides of the furniture piece and add 13" to each dimension. If you are matching pattern motifs add the inch measurement for one repeat to each measurement. (See Chapter Three, page 69.) Measure from the floor to the skirtline and add 2".

2. Follow Steps 3-5 for the Tailored Skirt with Corner Kick Pleats.

3. Following the instructions in Step 6 for the Tailored Skirt with Corner Kick Pleats, page 113, mark the pleats on each corner. Draw a center line on the front and back skirt sections and use these lines to mark the center pleats.

4. Finish the skirt following the instructions in Steps 7-10 for the Tailored Skirt with Corner Kick Pleats. Snip open seam line of the center pleat below the back closure and finish the edges following Step 3 for the gathered skirt, page 112. Repin the pleat before sewing on the skirt.

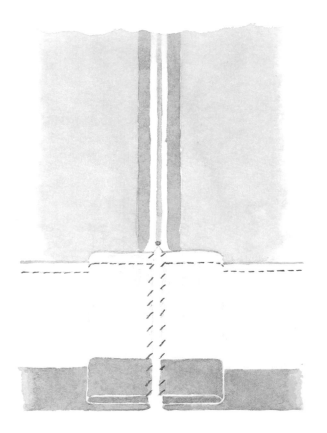

FIGURE 5

strips as you need to make up a skirt to these measurements.

2. Cut and stitch the lining and skirt sections together following Steps 4-5 for the Tailored Skirt with Corner Kick Pleats, page 113.

3. Starting at a seam, mark the box pleats at 3″ intervals around the skirting on the lining side. Label the marks A, B, C, B, A, repeating for each pleat. The last sequence may not be symmetrical, but this will be adjusted later.

4. With the skirt right side up, make each box pleat by pinching the A marks together and folding on the B mark (Figure 1). Pin to secure. If the last pleat is incomplete, leave it unpinned.

5. Place the slipcover on the furniture piece. With the right side out, slip the skirt over the furniture piece. Pin to secure at the skirtline. Adjust so the first complete box pleat is at the center front. If there is a closure in the body of the slipcover, align one of the skirt seamlines with it. The size of the pleats in between may need to be adjusted accordingly. Continue around the furniture piece. As you approach the last pleat, decrease the depth of the pleats to give the last pleat more fullness if needed. Increase the depth of the nearby pleats if the slack needs to be taken up.

6. Finish the skirt following steps 9-10 for the Tailored Skirt with Corner Kick Pleats.

tailored skirt with box pleats

This skirt has continuous pleats all the way around. Do not attempt to match pattern motifs, as the continuous folds make this impossible.

1. Measure the skirtline all the way around and multiply by three. Add 6″. Measure from the floor to the skirtline and add 2″. Cut as many

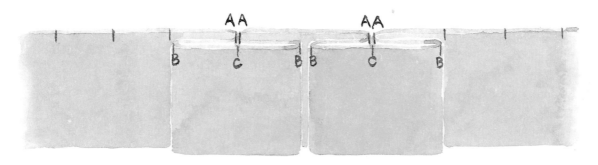

FIGURE 3
box pleats

box cushions

The seat and back cushions used on most upholstered furniture have sides, or boxing, and are known as box cushions. The seams are usually stitched with welting for a tailored look. If you are making an extra-long cushion, such as a sofa seat, you may have to piece it down the middle.

If your box cushions have lost their bounce, it is wise to replace them before slipcovering. When buying feather cushions, opt for a high-feather, low-down ratio; all-down cushions will be too soft. You can also buy polyester foam cut to size. Cushions 2″ thick are recommended for dining and side chairs, while 3″–4″ thick cushions are better for larger furniture pieces.

High density foam, which is more stable than normal density foam, is best for a long cushion because it is less likely to sag with use. A 2″ thick piece of high-density foam placed on the deck of a furniture piece under the slipcover will also provide cushions with additional support.

In addition to your fabric, you will need a zipper (the heavy industrial type with metal teeth is recommended). To determine the zipper length, measure the length of the back boxing piece. Add 6″ and round up to the nearest standard size.

Top and Bottom: Measure from front seam to back seam and add 1″. Measure from side seam to side seam and add 1″. Cut two fabric sections to these dimensions. Fold each in half twice and steam press the creases.

Boxing: Measure the length and the width of the cushion top. Add these two numbers together, then add 1″. Measure the height of the boxing and add 1″. Cut one section according to these measurements. This will be the front boxing strip. Repeat for the back boxing strip, but add 1½″ to the height to accommodate a zipper (Figure 1).

If there is welting, stitch it all the way around the top and bottom fabric sections. Fold the back boxing strip lengthwise and steam press the crease.

FIGURE 1

116

Fold the strip end to end and crease again. Cut along the lengthwise crease. Stitch the zipper between the two halves of this strip. (See Placket Zipper, Chapter Six, pages 141–142.) After the zipper is installed, stitch over the basted seam line on either end of the zipper. Sew the back boxing strip to the front boxing strip end to end to make a continuous round.

Attaching the Top, Bottom, and Boxing: Slip the boxing over the bottom of the cushion with the wrong side out. Center the seams of the boxing at the sides of the cushion. Mark each boxing corner with a vertical line. Remove the boxing and steam press at the pencil marks to make a fold at each corner. Align the center crease of the boxing with the center crease of the cushion top fabric section and pin at the corner creases. Open the zipper. Sew the two sections together. Repeat to sew on the bottom section. Turn the cover right side out.

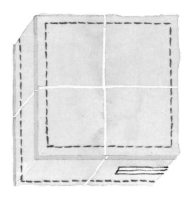

attaching the boxing

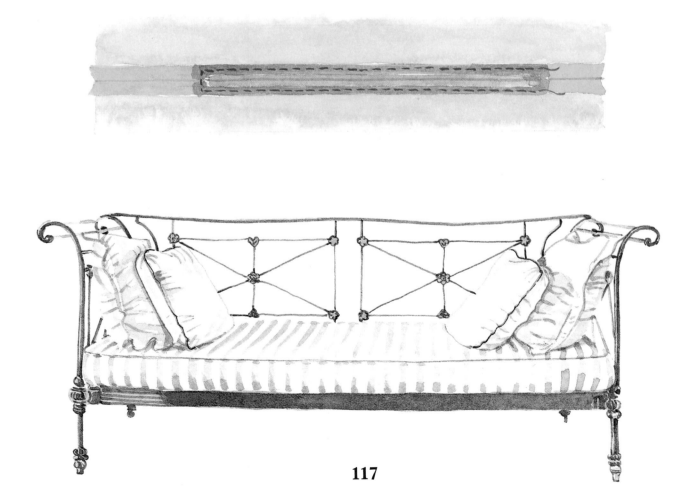

117

shaped box cushions

Some cushions are rounded or T-shaped. These require a pattern.

Top and Bottom: Place the cushion on a sheet of paper and trace around it with a pencil. Draw a line ½″ out from the tracing line and cut. Cut a top and bottom fabric section using this pattern.

Boxing: Measure all the way around the boxing with a cloth tape measure and add 2″. Divide the total in half. Measure the boxing height and add 1″. Cut 1 section according to these measurements. This will be the front boxing strip. Repeat for the back boxing strip, but add 1½″ to the height to accommodate a zipper.

Attaching the Top, Bottom, and Boxing: If there is welting, stitch it all the way around the top and bottom fabric sections. Assemble the boxing and install the zipper as for Box Cushions. Open the zipper. Stitch the top edge of the boxing to the top cushion piece. Sitch the bottom edge of the boxing to the bottom. Turn the cover inside out.

bolsters

This basic round bolster cover is made from three fabric sections and closed with slipstitching.

Body: Measure the bolster from end seam to end seam and add 1″. Measure the circumference and add 1″. Cut one body section to these measurements.

Ends: Measure the diameter of one end and add 1″. Cut two circular sections to this diameter. (For instructions on how to do this, see Step 3 in the Ruffled Pillow Round, Chapter Four, page 96.) Staystitch around the edges of both circular sections.

Attaching the Body and Ends: Fold the body section in half lengthwise with the right sides together to create a tube. Stitch the seam along the length, leaving a 6″ gap in the center for a closure. If there is welting, stitch it around each end of the tube. With the right sides together, sew a circular section onto each end of the tube, easing and clipping around the curves. Trim the seams. Turn the case right side out. Insert the bolster and slipstitch the closure to secure.

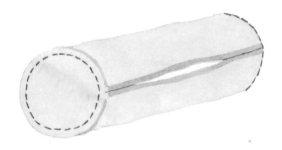

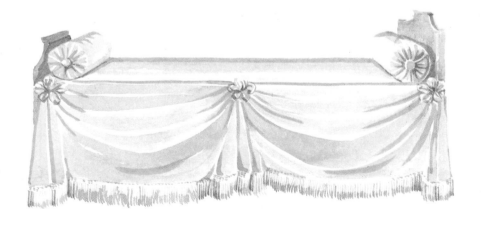

arm protectors

Measure the furniture arm on the outside, from just under the scroll to 6″ above the cushion on the inside arm. Add 1″. Measure the furniture arm from front to back. Add 1″. Cut two fabric sections to these dimensions. Turn under the edges of each section ¼″ all the way around and steam press. Turn under the creased edges another ¼″, steam press, and topstitch. Place a protector on each arm and slipstitch to the furniture piece at each corner.

final fitting

Slip on the cover, first over the back of the furniture, then over one arm, and then the other, smoothing it over the shoulders and arm fronts. Using a ruler, tuck in the fabric around the deck and between the back and arm. If there is an opening in the skirt beneath the closure, slipstitch it closed. Insert T-pins in crucial spots like the corners, skirtline, and under the arm scrolls or other curved details. Steam press the slipcover right on the piece of furniture.

maintaining your slipcover

Slipcovers are designed to be cleaned as frequently as necessary. Launder or dry clean according to the results of your fabric testing in Chapter Three. If you are laundering, always remove the slipcover from the dryer while it is still damp, place it on the furniture piece, and steam press it until dry. Always dry clean a cover that has trim.

terms and techniques A to Z

Throughout this volume, you will encounter numerous references to sewing terms and techniques. In many cases, these are the same as they would be in regular dressmaking directions but not always. For example, the standard seam allowance in dressmaking is ⅝", but in slipcovering it is ½". No matter how good your sewing skills, be sure to consult this chapter whenever you encounter a particular term in order to prevent any mistaken assumptions. For easy reference, the terms and techniques appear in alphabetical order.

applique

An applique is a cut-out fabric motif stitched to another, larger piece of background fabric; it might also be a piece of needlework or lace. In slipcovering, appliques are most commonly used on a pillow or cushion front.

finished-edge applique

If your applique already has finished edges, it can be attached without any special preparation.

1. Position the applique with the right side up on the top of the background fabric, smooth the surface, and pin around the edges.

2. Stitch all around the edge of the applique using a tiny blanket stitch. Ease the stitching around corners, removing the pins as you go.

raw-edge applique

Adding a border of applied trim or ribbon with mitered corners is a good way to conceal the raw edges of an unfinished applique.

1. Position the applique with the right side up on the background fabric, smooth the surface, and pin in place.

2. Fold under the end of the ribbon ½″ and pin to one corner of the applique, overlapping the edge a bit, depending on how much of the applique you want covered by the ribbon.

3. Pin the ribbon along the first edge of the applique. When you reach the the next corner, overlap a bit, then fold the ribbon back on itself with the edges aligned (Figure 1). Pin the fold at the bottom. To miter the corner, fold the ribbon on the diagonal (on the dotted line), steam press, and pin (Figure 2). (It would also be helpful to sew the mitered corner with a few slipstitches along the dotted line.) Continue pinning the ribbon, folding in the same manner at the two remaining corners.

4. To join the ends, pin the ribbon all the way to the corner and trim so it is flush with the edge (Figure 3). Fold the trimmed end under on the diagonal and pin in place.

5. Slipstitch both edges of the ribbon to the applique and background fabric, beginning with the outer edge. Remove the pins as you progress.

FIGURE 1

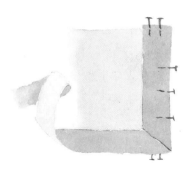

FIGURE 2

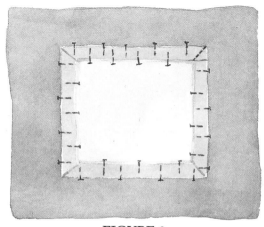

FIGURE 3

hemmed-edge appliqué

This technique works well for an unfinished square or rectangular appliqué with raw edges.

1. With the appliqué wrong side up staystitch all the way around, ¼″ from the edge.

2. Miter the corners. Fold back each corner at the point where the staystitching intersects and steam press (Figure 1). Fold each edge back along the staystitching lines (Figure 2), forming a point at each corner. Steam press.

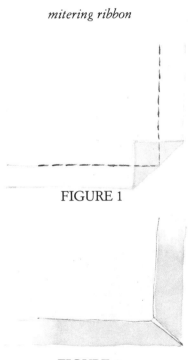

mitering ribbon

FIGURE 1

FIGURE 2

3. Position the appliqué right side up on the background fabric and pin in place around the edges. Machine stitch all the way around the edges, using a zig-zag stitch or special appliqué foot; or work all around the edges by hand with a blanket stitch. Remove the pins.

curved-hem appliqué

Hemming a curved appliqué requires clipping the edges of the fabric.

1. With the appliqué wrong side up staystitch all the way around, ¼″ from the edge.

2. Carefully fold over the edges, steam pressing and clipping as you go; the clipped areas of the edges will overlap to adjust to the curve.

3. To apply the appliqué, follow the instructions in Step 3 for hemmed-edged appliqué.

backstitch

In backstitching, one side of the seam looks like straight machine stitching; on the reverse side, the stitches overlap. This stitching is recommended for hand-sewn seams because it is so strong.

1. Place the sections to be joined with the right sides together. Knot the thread and pull the needle through the fabric at the point on the seam line where you wish to begin sewing. Insert the needle ⅛″ behind that point on the seam line, and pull it down through the fabric.

2. Still working on the seam line, bring the needle up through the fabric ¼″ in front of the first stitch and insert it again at the point where the needle first came out. Continue stitching in this manner, always inserting the needle into the hole made by the previous stitch.

Backstitch

basting

Basting is loose stitching used to make a temporary seam or to gather fabric.

Machine basting is done with the stitch length selector set to the minimum number of stitches per inch (usually 4–6) and with the upper tension on the tension regulator reduced.

Hand basting is done as a line of loose running stitches, which makes it easy to secure several layers of fabric—particularly sections that have been gathered or that need to be eased. When hand basting pattern sections over a piece of furniture during pattern making, use thread in an easy-to-see contrasting color. Other basting, by machine or by hand, calls for matching thread, since the basting stitches are not usually removed.

bias

The bias runs diagonal to the lengthwise grain of the fabric.

blanket stitch

This stitch is used as an edging for raw fabric, as when securing an appliqué to a piece of background fabric.

1. Position the appliqué right side up on the background fabric, smooth the surface, and pin. Secure the thread at the left end of the edge you wish to sew by making a tiny stitch on the wrong side of the appliqué. Bring the needle out just under the edge of the appliqué.

2. Insert the needle ¼″ in from the appliqué edge, piercing both the appliqué and background fabric. Hold the bottom part of the thread in a loop.

3. Bring the needle up again on the appliqué edge, catching the thread loop with the tip. Pull the needle through, forming a bar at the appliqué edge. Again insert the needle ¼″ in from the appliqué edge, a short distance from the first stitch. Bring the needle out at the bottom, again catching it in a loop of thread. Repeat, placing your stitches at even intervals.

Blanket Stitch

buttons and buttonholes

Buttons and buttonholes can be used to close a pillow cover, and they also make a decorative finishing touch for a sofa or chair cover.

1. With the right sides up, overlap the faced edges of the two sections to be joined by 1″ and secure with pins. Determine the placement for each button (at least ¼″ in from the edge) and mark with a dot.

2. Beginning with the centermost mark, push a pin through the top section and facing, and, lifting up the top section slightly, mark the point where it pierces the bottom section with a dot. Repeat for all button marks.

3. Unpin the two sections, position a button over each mark on the bottom section, and sew it on.

4. Overlap the faced edges of the sections again as in Step 1, and re-pin with the top section lying flat over the buttons. Center each dot over a button. Lightly pencil a horizontal line over each button imprint on either side of the dot.

5. With a small pair of sharp-tipped scissors, make tiny snips along the line to make a slit just long enough to fit over the button.

6. Work around the edges of each slit with buttonhole stitch.

buttonhole stitch

This stitch is used to secure the raw edges of an eyelet or buttonhole. A line of staystitching serves as a guide.

buttons and buttonholes

1. On the right side of the fabric, use tiny running stitches to staystitch around the slit or eyelet hole ⅛″ from the edge. Be sure to stitch through all layers of fabric.

2. Secure the thread by making a tiny stitch on the wrong side of the fabric. Bring the needle up through the fabric from the wrong side, just above the staystitching line. Insert it through the opening directly below and bring it up again from the wrong side at the staystitching line, leaving a loop at the edge of the opening. Slip the needle up through the loop, and pull it taut. Insert the needle again through the slit, bring it out close to the previous stitch, catch the loop, and pull taut to make a tiny knot at the edge of the opening.

3. Repeat, placing each stitch so it touches the previous one. Fan the stitches gently to go around curves.

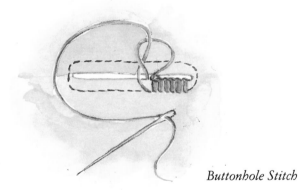

Buttonhole Stitch

clipping and trimming

Clipping and trimming fabric edges helps seams lie flat around corners and curves. To clip a convex curve, snip directly into the seam allowance with small, sharp-tipped scissors, cutting right up to the seam stitching, but not into it. To clip a concave curve, snip a small, triangular notch in the same manner. Unless otherwise indicated, all clips and notches are spaced at 1″ intervals, and all trimming is to ¼″. Corners are trimmed with a diagonal cut.

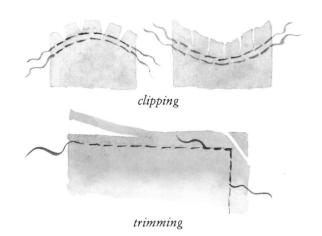

clipping

trimming

closures

While a zipper is traditional, there are many alternative closures for pillow cases and slipcovers. Your choice will depend on the fabric you are using, the size and placement of the opening, and whether you want the closure to be purely functional, or to double as a decorative touch. Except for zippers, the directions for closures in this volume all involve joining two slipcover sections that have already been finished with a facing. (See Buttons and Buttonholes, Eyelets, Slipstitch, Snap Fasteners, Ties, Velcro™, and Zippers.)

cross stitch

Cross stitching is used for tacked-corner quilting and for hand shirring. Each cross stitch is worked as an X.

1. Work with the fabric right side up. Knot the thread and bring up the needle through the fabric from the wrong side. Insert the needle to form one diagonal of the X.

2. Bring the needle up again across from the bottom of the first stitch and cross over the diagonal to complete the X. To reinforce, make a second X over the first.

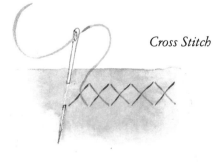

Cross Stitch

darts

Darts, or pointed tucks, are used to ease fullness at a curved edge without gathering.

1. Transfer the dart markings accurately to the wrong side of the fabric section. Fold the fabric with the right sides together so that the marked lines are aligned. Pin.

2. Stitch in a line from the wide end of the dart down to the point, sewing the last few stitches directly on the fold. If using a sewing machine, instead of reinforcing at the point, tie the two stitching threads into several knots.

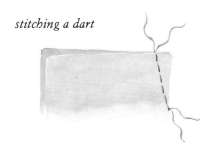

stitching a dart

easing

Easing is used to join two fabric sections whose seam lines are of unequal length.

1. Place the two sections to be joined with the right sides together and the longer section on top. Align the two ends of the seam lines and pin (Figure 1).

2. If the lengths of the two sections differ by only a few inches, you can ease in the extra fabric by pinning. Pin the two sections together at the center of the seam line. On one side of the center pin, pinch a little extra of the top section and secure with a pin on either side of the pinch (Figure 2). (Don't pin into the pinch.) Work on both sides of the center pin, until all the extra fabric has been eased in. Stitch slowly, removing the pins as you sew. Clip and trim the seam allowances.

FIGURE 1

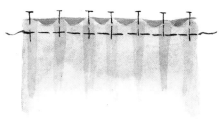

FIGURE 2

pin easing

3. If the amount to be eased is more than a few inches, gather the longer section first, following the instructions in Traditional Machine Gathering page 127. Pull the bobbin threads just enough so the longer section is the desired length.

4. To ease a curved edge to a straight one, staystitch along the curved edge and pin as in Step 2. Stitch slowly, removing the pins as you sew. Clip and trim the seam allowances.

eyelets

Lacing a cord through a series of eyelets is good for a loose or decorative closure, but will not work for fabric that is pulled together with any real tension. Lacing cord is sold along with other notions; ribbon or decorative cording can also be used.

1. Determine the placement you want for the eyelets, which should align on both sides of the closure—like the eyelets on a shoe—and mark each with a dot.

2. With a small pair of sharp-tipped scissors, make tiny snips around each dot, cutting

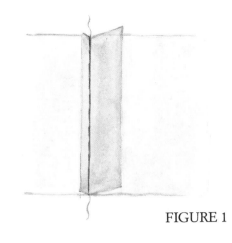

FIGURE 1

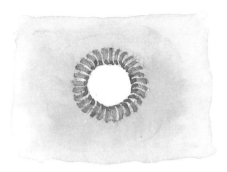

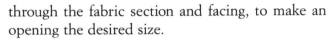

Eyelet

through the fabric section and facing, to make an opening the desired size.

3. Work around the edges of the opening with the buttonhole stitch, fanning the stitches around the curve. (You can also use commercially made metal eyelets that are tapped together over the eyelet hole.) Thread the cord or ribbon through the eyelets and tie them into a bow.

fabric

Fabric refers to the slipcover material itself. Other kinds of cloth are referred to by their use— for example, lining, facing, interfacing, and backing.

facing

A facing is a piece of fabric used to finish a raw edge. All of the closures for pillow covers and slipcovers, except those for zippers, are faced. Directions appear in individual projects.

flat felled seam

A flat felled seam, which has a finished edge, is recommended for transparent fabrics and those prone to raveling. On the right side, the seam will appear as two neat lines of parallel stitching.

1. Stitch two fabric sections together with a normal seam and steam press the seam allowance open (Figure 1). With the wrong side of the fabric up, trim one side of the seam allowance to ⅛″.

2. Fold the raw edge of the untrimmed seam allowance under ⅛″ and press (Figure 2).

3. Press the trimmed seam allowance toward the folded seam allowance (Figure 3).

4. Fold the folded edge over the trimmed edge and steam press flat. Topstitch along the edge of the fold (Figure 4).

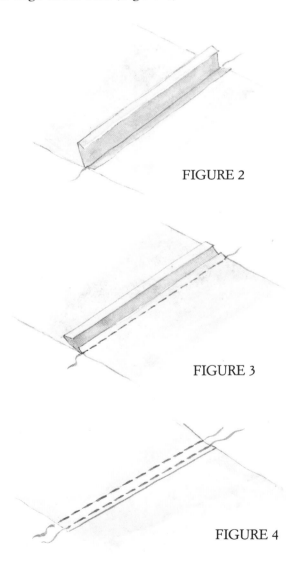

FIGURE 2

FIGURE 3

FIGURE 4

gathering

Gathering is particularly useful for easing fabric around a corner, or for fitting a curved section, such as the front of an arm, to another section. It is also used to make ruffles.

If you have a gathering foot for your sewing machine, the job will be done automatically as the needle takes up each stitch. If you do not have one of these attachments, use one of the following methods.

traditional machine gathering

This simple technique involves sewing two lines of loose stitching; when the bottom (bobbin) thread is pulled, the fabric is caught into gathers.

1. Adjust the stitch-length selector on your sewing machine to 4–6 stitches per inch (basting length), and reduce the upper tension on the tension regulator.

2. With the fabric right side up, sew two parallel lines along the section you wish to gather, beginning and ending ½" into the seam line (Figure 1). Leave a 3" tail of thread at either end and do not reinforce the stitching lines. The first stitching line should be directly on the ½" seam line, the second should be ¼" away, between the seam line and the edge of the fabric. Limit these lines to 24" or less, so the threads don't break when you pull them to gather. (If the gathering area is longer, stop at 24" and start a new line.) If you must cross over a seam, lift the seam allowance and sew under it, stopping a few stitches short of the seam. Then resume sewing under the seam allowance on the other side.

3. Gently pull the tails of the two bottom (bobbin) threads at one end of the double row of stitches. As the gathers form, push them carefully toward the center with your fingers. Repeat at the other end of the double row of stitches, adjusting the gathers until they are uniform and the desired fullness is achieved (Figure 2). To secure the threads temporarily, wind the tails of the threads around a pin at each end of the gathered section.

4. Adjust the stitch-length selector on your machine to 12–14 stitches per inch (normal length) and return the tension regulator to normal. With the gathered fabric right side up, sew a line of stitching between the two rows of gathering stitches. Stitch a second line directly on the seam line. Remove the pins.

Traditional Machine Gathering

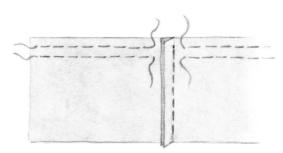

FIGURE 1

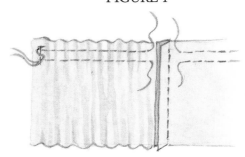

FIGURE 2

quick machine gathering

This one-step method of machine gathering involves forming the gathers with your fingers and securing them with stitching as you go. It is best for tight, full gathers.

1. Adjust the stitch-length selector on your machine to 12–14 stitches per inch (normal length). With the right side up, place the fabric on the machine and lower the needle into the ½" seam line at the point where you wish to begin gathering. Pinch 1" of the fabric in front of the needle into tight gathers. Keep the folds close together with your fingers, and slowly begin to stitch, applying steady pressure on the fabric in front of the needle (Figure 1). Moving forward 1″ at a time, continue stitching until the gathering is finished. Steam press the seam allowance flat. Sew a second line of stitching parallel to the first, ¼″ in from the fabric edge.

2. Adjust the gathering to the desired size. If it is too long, find places where the gathers can be tightened and stitch again. If it is too short, gently pull loose a few gathers every few inches by breaking the threads.

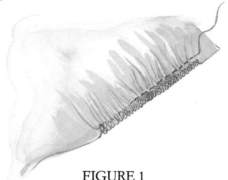

FIGURE 1
Quick Machine Gathering

grain

Fabric grain runs in two directions: the crosswise grain runs perpendicular to the selvages, and the lengthwise grain runs parallel to the selvages. The grain is straight when the crosswise and lengthwise grains meet at right angles.

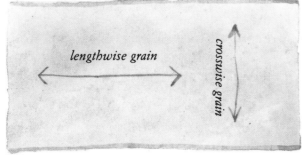

selvage

lengthwise grain

crosswise grain

hemstitch

Hemstitch is worked on the wrong side of the fabric, and is barely visible from the right side; if the fabric is lined or faced it is not visible at all.

1. Turn up the hem according to the directions in your specific project.

2. With the wrong side of the fabric facing up, knot the thread and pull the needle up at the edge of the hem just in from the fold.

3. Stitch, following the directions for Step 3 in slipstitching, page 135. Make the stitches as small as possible.

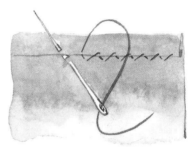

Hemstitch

interfacing

An interfacing is a piece of stiff fabric that is sandwiched between the facing and fabric to give shape and stability to small but crucial sections of a slipcover, such as a shoulder or an arm front.

The interfacing piece is cut to match the facing, minus the ½″ seam allowances. It is then basted or fused with a hot iron to the wrong side of the slipcover section before the facing is attached. Interfacing fabric is available at fabric stores and comes in a variety of weights. Choose one that is closest to the weight of the slipcover fabric.

patterns

Primary sections of armchair, sofa, and chaise slipcovers call for cloth patterns made from bed sheets or muslin (see Chapter Three). It is not necessary to make cloth patterns for most cushions, ottomans, daybeds, or slipper chairs. When specific projects call for paper patterns, use brown wrapping paper.

quilting

Quilting, which involves sandwiching a layer of

soft batting between a top fabric and a backing, provides extra body in a slipcover. It can also be very economical, as it enables you to use sheeting and inexpensive lightweight cottons that would not hold up on their own. And, whereas unquilted fabric often sags if not properly eased and fitted, quilting takes up the slack and produces a remarkably smooth fit.

In general, only the fabric for the cushion tops and fronts, arms, and inside back of the slipcover—those areas that get the most wear—need to be quilted. When using lightweight fabrics and sheeting, the skirt and the outside back can be left unquilted, but should be lined.

To make the process easier, the slipcover sections are cut first, then quilted. For each section to be quilted, you need a piece of batting and a piece of backing, all cut to the same size as the fabric section. You can use your fabric patterns for the backing sections. These are ideal, as they already will have been marked. The batting can be cut from a sheet of polyester fiber, or from cotton or wool batting, which are more expensive.

general preparations

1. Prepare your pattern sections following the instructions in Chapter Three, pages 78–86; these will be your backing pieces. Set aside all sections that will not be quilted.

2. Using the pattern, cut a batting section and fabric section to the same size. (Begin with the cushion tops, then follow with the arm sections and the inside back section.)

3. Place the backing piece wrong side up and mark a seam line ½" in from the edge all the way around (Figure 1). Draw a second line ½" in from the first line all the way around as shown. You will be keeping all of your quilting stitches within this 1" margin.

4. Place your slipcover section flat with

the wrong side up. Place the batting piece on top, then place the backing piece over the batting with the wrong side up (Figure 2). Make sure the edges of all three pieces are aligned. Pin around the edges, then in the center, then every 3" or 4" over the entire surface. This keeps the layers anchored when you sew the pieces together.

FIGURE 1

FIGURE 2

channel quilting

Sewn in parallel lines, channel quilting works well with striped patterns and gives a luxurious look and feel to solid-color fabrics. Channeling also helps conceal piecing seams. The quilting can be done either by hand, using a running stitch, or by machine. Hand sewing takes longer but makes it much easier to keep the layers smooth as you sew.

1. Prepare your fabric sections, batting, and backing pieces following the instructions in General Preparations, opposite. Adjust the stitch-length selector on your machine to 4–6 stitches per inch (basting length) and reduce the upper tension on the tension regulator.

2. Decide how wide you want your channels to be (2"–4" intervals are recommended). Using a pencil and a yardstick, mark a series of parallel lines on the backing piece (Figure 3). Do not mark beyond the 1″ outer margin.

FIGURE 3

3. Begin by quilting the center channel line, stitching slowly with running stitches or machine stitching so that none of the layers are pulled, and taking care not to stitch beyond the 1″ outer margin. In the same manner, continue stitching along the parallel lines, alternating on either side of the center channel, continually checking to make sure the layers are smooth. Trim all threads.

tacked corner quilting

Tacked corner quilting requires minimal stitching—just enough to hold the layers of fabric and batting together. (It is not necessary to use batting if your fabric and backing have enough weight on their own.) Tacked corner quilting can be done by cross stitching over the intersecting lines of a grid, which is steam pressed into the fabric. The size of the grid is up to you—the tighter it is, the more cross stitching is required.

1. Steam press a grid into the backing piece, following the instructions in Chapter Three, page 79.

2. Prepare your slipcover sections, batting, and backing pieces following the directions in General Preparations, page 129.

3. Place the slipcover section with the backing side up. Make a small reinforced cross stitch at the centermost intersection of the grid. Snip the thread and re-knot for a new stitch. Continue in this manner, tacking each intersection with reinforced

cross stitches, working outward from the center (Figure 4). Do not stitch beyond the 1″ outer margin. As you work, keep checking the fabric side of the layered piece to make sure it is smooth. Trim all threads.

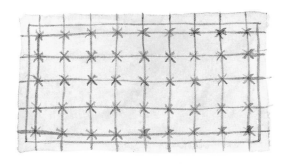

FIGURE 4

quilting around motifs

Quilting a fabric section with dominant motifs, like those on a floral-print chintz, enhances the design and gives a rich look to a slipcover.

1. Follow the instructions in Chapter Five, page 101, for centering the motifs on all the sections to be quilted.

2. Place the fabric section to be quilted with the right side up. Handstitch around the motif with running stitches, tracing its general shape (Figure 5). Randomly tack the centers of flowers or other points of interest with reinforced cross stitches. This will help anchor the fabric in areas between the outline of the design and the corners of the fabric section. Do not stitch beyond the 1″ outer margin. Trim all threads.

seaming a quilted section

1. Place the quilted piece flat, with the backing side up. Fold back the raw edges of the batting and backing along the inner marked line and pin. To reduce bulk, only the slipcover fabric will be sewn into the seam allowance (Figure 6).

2. Place the two sections to be seamed with the right sides together and pin at the seam line. Stitch. Remove the pins and steam press the seam allowance flat. Unpin the backing and batting piece and trim the raw edges back to the seamline.

FIGURE 5

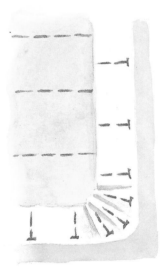

FIGURE 6

railroading

Fabric that has no design or nap (surface texture), or that has a nondirectional design, can be railroaded, or run horizontally over a piece of furni-

ture. This saves yardage and eliminates extra seams, especially on a large piece of furniture, such as a three-seat sofa, because the pattern pieces can be placed with their top and bottom edges parallel to either the crosswise or the lengthwise grain. On fabric with a nap or with a directional design, the pattern pieces must all be laid out in the same direction.

reinforcing

When starting and ending a seam, it is necessary to reinforce it for a few stitches to make sure it doesn't ravel. Corners are also reinforced to strengthen the seam line before clipping and turning. To reinforce, stitch forward ½", reverse and stitch ½", then continue to stitch forward along the seam line. Unless otherwise indicated, all seams are begun and finished in this manner.

repeat

A repeat is a pattern with a motif or motifs duplicated at exact intervals down the lengthwise grain of the yardage. Small pattern repeats can occur every few inches, but large pattern repeats can be as much as 12"–24" or more apart. To calculate the repeat, measure the distance between identical features in the design. Although a repeat of a few inches will not require much extra fabric, large repeats can considerably increase the amount needed. (See Chapter Three, page 69.)

running stitch

This is the simplest of hand stitches, but not the strongest. Therefore, it should not be used when the fabric is under tension. Large running stitches are used for hand basting.

1. Knot the thread, and working with the fabric right side up, bring the needle up from the wrong side to secure.

2. Slide (or run) the needle through the fabric, taking two or three stitches at a time. Draw the thread through and repeat until you have completed your line of stitching.

ruffles

A ruffle is essentially nothing more than a rectangular strip of fabric pulled into gathers. Because the gathers "use up" a considerable amount of fabric, you must start with a strip that is quite a bit longer than the finished ruffle. A ratio of 3 to 1 is recommended for full ruffles; this may require piecing sections of fabric together to make a strip that is long enough.

For proper body and shape, a ruffle needs a backing. If only one side is going to show, as in a chair skirt, a normal lining will suffice. If both sides of a ruffle are visible, as for a pillow trim, the ruffle should be self-faced.

lined ruffle

1. To calculate the length of fabric strip needed, first measure the circumference or length of the section where the ruffle will be attached. Multiply that measurement by three. Determine the width of the finished ruffle and add 2″. Calculate the measurement for the lining in the same manner, but add only 1″ to the width dimension.

2. On the straight grain, cut a single strip of fabric to your measurements, or sew together several lengths with ½″ seams to make up a single strip, and steam press the seams open. (If your fabric has a directional pattern, be sure to cut the strip or pieces from selvage to selvage.)

3. With the right sides together, align the bottom edges of the fabric strip and the lining piece, pin, and stitch with a ½″ seam. Steam press the seams open. Remove the pins.

4. Place the fabric strip flat with the wrong side up, and pull the lining up so that its top raw edge aligns with the top raw edge of the fabric strip (Figure 1). At the bottom of the lining piece, 1″

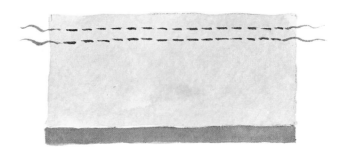

FIGURE 1
Lined Ruffle

of fabric will now show.

5. Stitch along the seam line at the top edges to secure the lining. Steam press the bottom edge to create a sharp crease; this will be the hem.

6. Treating the fabric and lining as one piece, gather at the top edge, following the instructions for Quick Machine Gathering, page 127, or Machine Shirring, pages 134–135.

7. If you are making a continuous ruffle to encircle a pillow or to form a skirt, you will need to join the ends before you attach it. With the right sides together, align the raw edges of the short ends and stitch a ½″ seam. Steam press the seams open.

self-faced ruffle

The fabric strip for a self-faced ruffle is cut doubly wide, then folded lengthwise so that the finished ruffle shows fabric on both sides.

1. To calculate the length of fabric strip needed to make your ruffle, measure the circumference or length of the section to which the ruffle will be attached. Multiply that measurement by three. Determine the width of the finished ruffle, double that measurement, and add 1″ for the seam allowance.

2. On the straight grain, cut a strip of fabric to your measurements, or sew together several lengths with ½″ seams to make up a single strip, and steam press the seams open. (If your fabric has a directional pattern, be sure to cut the strips or pieces from selvage to selvage.)

3. With the wrong sides together, fold the fabric strip in half lengthwise and steam press the fold, which will form the hem of the ruffle.

4. Treating the two fabric layers as one, gather the top edge following the instructions in Quick Machine Gathering, page 127.

seaming a gathered section or ruffle

Seaming a ruffle or gathered section to another section takes care, as it is important not to catch any of the gathers in your seam line.

1. Place the ruffle or gathered piece and the section it will be seamed to right sides together, with the gathered section on top. Pin through the seam line to secure (Figure 2).

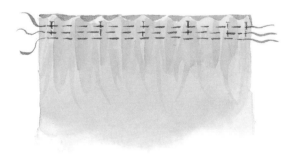

FIGURE 2

2. If you are an inexperienced machine sewer, hand baste the two sections together along the seam line with the same thread that is in your machine. This will hold the sections together during machine stitching and will help keep the gathers from catching. If you are going around a corner, ease

the extra fullness. Pin the bunched gathers away from the seam to prevent them from getting caught in the seam (Figure 3).

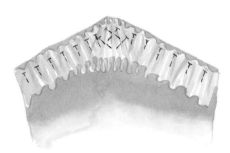

FIGURE 3
easing around a corner

3. Stitch along the seam line. If you have not basted, remove the pins as you sew. (The basting can remain.)

4. Stitch the gathered seam a second time, ¼″ from the fabric edge. This second line helps the gathers fall in folds instead of splaying open. Clip the threads, and steam press the seam allowances away from the gathered edge.

seam

Stitching an even seam is fundamental to any successful sewing project. If you are a beginner, it is a good idea to baste along the seam line before you stitch. Otherwise, use the pin-and-stitch method described. Unless otherwise indicated, all seams are stitched with the stitch length selector on your machine set at 12–14 inches (normal length) and the tension regulator set to normal.

1. Place the two sections to be joined right sides together. Pin, placing the pins perpendicular to the seam line with the heads to the right.

2. Begin stitching ½″ in from the end of the seam line. Reinforce, then stitch the length of the seam, stopping ½″ from the end. Reinforce again. Remove the pins as you go.

seam allowance

The seam allowance is the amount of fabric used to make a seam and must be added into your calculations when cutting each slipcover section. For example, to make a pillow case 20″ square, using a ½″ seam allowance, you will need to cut a 21″ fabric square. This takes into account a ½″ seam allowance on each side.

seam line

The seam line is the line along which two fabric sections are sewn to make a seam. All seams are stitched ½″ in from the edge of the sections unless otherwise indicated.

sections

Sections are the individual fabric pieces that are cut to size and joined together at their corresponding edges to make a slipcover.

selvages

The finished edges woven into fabric to keep it from raveling are called selvages. Useful information such as repeat marks, fiber content, cleaning instructions, color swatches, a designer's name, and the word "colorfast" can be found printed in these narrow borders.

shirring (hand)

Hand shirring, or gathering a seam with groups of cross stitches, is recommended for a two-sided round pillow cover. No matter how much you clip and press the curved seam, it won't be smooth; so rather than fight the pucker, you can enhance it with shirring, which will create a uniform pouf.

1. Clip and press open the seam you intend to shirr. With the fabric wrong side up, sew a cross stitch over the seam and reinforce it with a second stitch. Without cutting the thread, make three more cross stitches at ½″ intervals.

2. After you make the fourth cross stitch, pull the thread to gather the seam into a pucker. Adjust to the desired fullness, then reinforce the fourth cross stitch to secure.

3. Continue in the same manner around the seam, four stitches at a time, adjusting the resulting pouf to the desired fullness as you go.

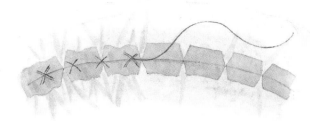

Hand-Shirred Seam

shirring (machine)

Machine shirring, which produces fine, deep gathers, involves using a special tape. The tape is stitched to the fabric on either side of parallel cords; when the cords are pulled, the fabric is caught into gathers. Gathering multiple rows is much too difficult to attempt without shirring tape, but quite simple with it because the cords are much sturdier to pull than bobbin threads. The tape also makes it much easier to gather heavyweight fabrics and those with a pile or nap. Shirring tape is available with as many as eight rows of cord; buy the soft kind, without a stiff backing.

1. Adjust the stitch-length selector on your machine to 12–14 stitches per inch (normal length).

2. Place your fabric section wrong side up and cut the shirring tape to the same measurement as the edge of the section to be gathered. Place the tape on the fabric right side up, aligning the top edge with the edge of the fabric. With the pins perpendicular, pin along the top cord.

3. Slowly stitch a line above and below the cord, directly over the stitching lines marked on the tape, removing the pins as you go. Repeat for all the cords. Secure each cord at one end by stitching across it, leaving the opposite end free.

4. At the free end, gently pull each cord until the shirring is the required length. To secure, wind the tail of each cord around a pin.

5. If you are shirring both the top and bottom of a fabric section, stitch the shirring tape to the bottom edge exactly as you did to the top.

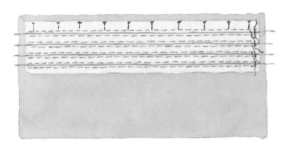

Machine Shirring

slipstitch

Slipstitching is used to secure two faced or folded section edges, which may overlap or abut. It is worked on the right sides of the fabric.

1. For overlapping sections, place the sections right sides up and overlap them the desired amount. Knot the thread and bring the needle up from the wrong side of the top section just in from the faced edge.

2. Take a small diagonal stitch, catching a few threads of the fabric underneath. Taking another small diagonal stitch, bring the needle up, close to the edge of the top section as before. Continue in this manner, spacing the stitches at ⅛″ intervals.

3. For abutting sections, place the sections edge to edge and stitch as in Step 1.

slipstitched closure

Although large cushion covers would be a nuisance to close by hand stitching, it can work well for a small throw pillow where a stiff zipper might be undesirable. If you use this method, you will have to snip the stitching and re-sew every time you remove and replace the cover.

1. Place the sections to be joined with the right sides up, aligning the faced edges so they abut or overlap (depending on what the specific project calls for), and pin. Slipstitch the edges together, remove the pins, and steam press.

2. If one section is edged with welting, fold under the raw edges of the unwelted section ½″ on the seam line and steam press. Align the folded edge with the welting casing seam line and pin. Slipstitch the fold to the seam line of the welting. Remove the pins.

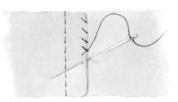

Overlapping Closure

Abutting Closure

slipstitching a welted seam

snap fasteners

Also called grippers, these fasteners are the kind commonly used on cowboy shirts and children's pajamas. Snap fasteners are not suitable for thin fabrics, but work very well for heavy fabrics. They are visible, however, and should be limited to areas that won't be seen.

Snap fasteners consist of three pieces: a stud, a socket, and a prong; there is sometimes a decorative prong as well. They come in packaged sets.

1. To position the snaps, follow Steps 1 and 2 in Buttons and Buttonholes, pages 123–124.

2. Using your placement marks, install the snaps following the manufacturer's directions. (You will need a wooden spool to tap the pieces together. If you only have plastic spools, buy a wooden spool of thread to have on hand.)

staystitch

Staystitching is a line of stitches sewn through a single layer of fabric. This is essential for curved edges that will be clipped or eased when seamed, or for an edge that is cut on the bias. Staystitching is done on the seam line; when the fabric section is seamed to another section, you can sew the seam directly over the staystitching line.

steam press

Pressing open the seam allowance after a seam is stitched ensures a flat, nicely defined line. Keep your ironing board, a good steam iron, spray mister, and damp pressing cloth handy: if there is one secret to success in slipcovering, it is to follow the directions for steam pressing at every stage of assembly.

ties

Narrow fabric ties are good for securing a seat cushion to a dining or side chair and can also be tied into decorative bows. Used in pairs, they are sewn into a closure facing or into the seam line of a cushion bottom before it is seamed.

1. Determine the length of each tie, adding extra length if the ties are to be made into a bow. If the ties are to be sewn into a seam, add ½″ for the seam allowance. For each tie, cut two strips of fabric as long as this measurement and ¾″ wide.

2. Place one strip with the wrong side up and fold one long edge up and over ¼″ and steam press. Repeat on the other long edge. With the wrong sides together, fold the strip in half lengthwise, aligning the folded edges. Steam press, and topstitch as close as possible to the folded edges. Repeat for all the strips.

attaching closure ties

1. Align the raw edges of the two sections of fabric to be closed, right sides up, and mark a dot where you want each pair of ties. Pin the ties in place. Stitch over them on the seam line, reinforcing several times (Figure 1). Remove the pins.

2. Place one section and its facing right sides together with the raw edges aligned and the ties (one of each pair) sandwiched in between (Figure 2).

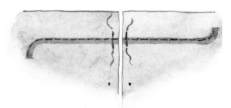

FIGURE 1

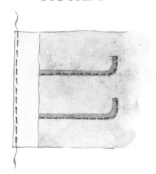

FIGURE 2

3. Stitch on the seam line and trim the seam allowance. Steam press the seam allowance to the wrong side. Fold the facing and section wrong sides together and topstitch ¼″ from the edge. Repeat for the second section and facing.

attaching seat cushion ties

1. Place the section for the seat cushion bottom on the chair, wrong side up, and mark the points where you want the ties to encircle the leg or post with dots.

2. Pin the ties so that their ends align with the edge of the fabric section. Stitch over them on the seam line, reinforcing several times. Remove the pins.

3. Pin together the boxing strip or the seat cushion top and the seat cushion bottom right sides together, sandwiching the ties, and stitch along the seam line. Remove the pins.

topstitching

This is a finishing stitch, sewn on the right side of the fabric.

1. To topstitch a seam, steam press the seam allowances flat toward one side of the seam.

2. Turn the fabric right side up and machine stitch ¼″ from the seam over the seam allowances.

trim application

With few exceptions, trims are applied in one of two ways. Welting and most ruffles are actually incorporated into the slipcover as part of a seam. Such decorative edgings as braid, ribbon, cording, fringe, lace, and piping, on the other hand, are usually stitched directly onto the surface of the slipcover fabric, often over a seam line. (Piping gives the same tailored definition as welting but without the bulk, and is a good choice to use with fabric that is

too thick to allow for the extra layers a welted seam requires.) The ends of any trim should start and finish in an unobtrusive place on the slipcover. In most cases, flat trim may be stitched along the edges by machine, but cording needs to be hand stitched.

general instructions

1. To attach trim to a finished seam, clip, and trim the seam allowance and steam press it open.

2. Turn the fabric right side up and pin the trim over the seam. Snip the ends, leaving a 1″ tail at each end.

3. Stitch the trim in place. If you are working with cording, turn the fabric wrong side up. Insert a threaded needle through the seam line and catch a few threads of the underside of the trim. Slipstitch in this manner along the entire length of the seam.

4. If you are not applying the trim over a seam, place it on the fabric as you like, and attach it with machine or hand stitching as above.

5. Finish the tails, following one of the methods below.

trim finishing

flat finish

Any trim that is thin enough to be folded under without creating extra bulk can be finished in this simple manner.

1. When you stitch the trim, fold over the beginning end ½″ and tuck under, securing as you stitch (Figure 1).

2. Trim the second tail to ½″. Fold under until the two ends of the trim abut. Secure with slipstitching (Figure 2).

FIGURE 1

FIGURE 2

tucked finish

Some cloth trim is double- or two-sided, so that the ends can be finished by neatly tucking one into the other. Work on the right side of the fabric.

1. Curl the raw edge of one tail under ¼″ and press in place with your fingers (Figure 3).

2. Insert the unfolded tail into the folded tail and slipstitch to secure (Figure 4).

3. On the wrong side of the fabric, stitch the gap in the seam line closed. Steam press.

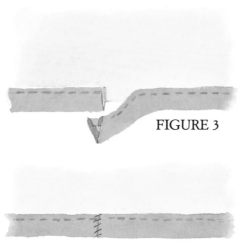

FIGURE 3

FIGURE 4

cording ends

Cording ends can be finished by neatly tucking them into a seam. Twisted cording needs special handling, as it starts to untwist as soon as it is cut; be sure to keep the ends taped to prevent this.

1. Snip a few stitches to make a small gap in the seam you are covering with the cord. Poke both 1″ cording tails through to the wrong side (Figure 5).

2. Turn the fabric wrong side up, and slipstitch the two tails to secure (Figure 6). Stitch the seam closed, reinforcing over the cord. Trim the tails.

FIGURE 5

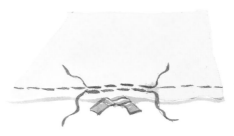

FIGURE 6

tassels and rosettes

In most cases, you can simply position these ornaments and attach them with slipstitching. They are are also useful for concealing the point where cording is joined, as in the following directions.

1. Turn the fabric right side up. If the cording is not too bulky, you can leave the tails free. Trim them so that they overlap by ¼″ (Figure 7).

2. Center the ornament over the tails and slipstitch all around to secure.

FIGURE 7

velcro ™

Velcro strips, which consist of two tapes that fuse when pressed together, are an excellent alternative to the long zippers needed for slipcover closures. Velcro also makes a good closure for fold-over flaps, but is too bulky for most pillow covers and lightweight fabrics.

1. Overlap the faced edges of the two sections to be joined by 1″ and determine the placement for the velcro strip.

2. Apply the strips according to the manufacturer's directions. You can secure the bottom strip with machine stitching, but slipstitch the top strip to the facing; otherwise the stitches will be visible on the right side of the top section.

welting

This finishing trim consists of soft cording covered with a fabric casing that is stitched right into a seam. It enhances the look and fit of a slipcover, defines the seams, and conceals the stitching.

Commercially made welting is available by the yard, but the cording is often thin and skimpy, and the color selection limited. Making your own welting is less expensive, and enables you to use the fabric you want for the casing. If you desire welting covered in the same fabric as your slipcovering (known as self-welting), you have no choice but to make your own. You can buy cord by the yard. Suitable diameters for use in slipcovering run from ¼″ (standard welting), to ⅜″ and even ½″ for an exaggerated look.

For most people, defining every seam line with welting is overdoing it. Once you have made a few yards of welting, you can outline the sections in question and let your eye decide. To determine the total amount of cord you need, measure each section to be welted and take the sum of all the calculations. To determine the yardage required for the casing, see Chapter Three, page 69. Buy the cord in a single length, and keep it that way, coiling it neatly on the floor as you sew on the casing. Do not cut the welting into pieces until you are ready to stitch it into a seam.

cutting bias strips

The fabric casing is made from strips of fabric cut on the bias. The diagonal seams minimize bulk when the welting is stitched into a slipcover seam.

1. Prepare the fabric according to the instructions in Chapter Three, pages 77–78. It is important that the grain is straight before you proceed.

2. Determine the width of your bias strips. If your cord is ¼″ in diameter, cut strips 1⅝″ wide. If your cord is ⅜″ in diameter, cut strips 1¾″ wide. If your cord is ½″ in diameter, cut strips 2″ wide.

3. Place the fabric wrong side up and make a diagonal fold (Figure 1). Cut along the fold. This is the true bias, and your guide for marking the cutting lines for bias strips.

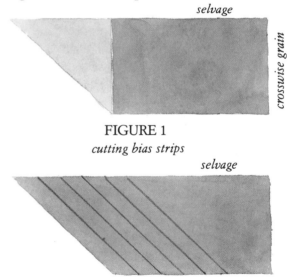

selvage

crosswise grain

FIGURE 1

cutting bias strips

selvage

FIGURE 2

4. With a yardstick and a pencil, mark parallel cutting lines from selvage to selvage according to the width you have determined in Step 2 (Figure 2). Cut out the strips.

5. Place the ends of two strips with the right sides together. Stitch them together on the diagonal with a ¼″ seam (Figure 3). Steam press the seam allowance open. Repeat to create one long fabric strip; this will be the welting casing.

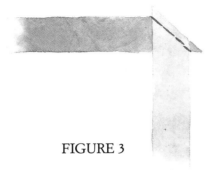

FIGURE 3

encasing the cord

1. Place the casing strip wrong side up and lay the cord lengthwise down the center. Fold the casing over the cord, align the raw edges, and pin the first few inches (Figure 4).

2. Adjust your stitch regulator to 4–6 inches (basting length). Using a zipper foot, stitch along the cord, staying as close to it as possible without sewing into it. Gently stretch the bias strips as you sew to make a smooth casing. This stitching creates a welting seam allowance.

FIGURE 4

sewing welting into a seam

1. Place one of the slipcover sections that is to be seamed with the right side up.

2. Align the raw edges of the welting seam allowance with the raw edges of the seam line

of the slipcover section and pin. If you need to go around a sharp corner, notch the edges of the casing at the point where it will turn the corner. (Figures 5 and 6.) A softer corner is made by making several clips at the point where the welting turns the corner (Figures 7 and 8).

FIGURE 5

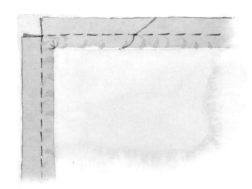

FIGURE 6

FIGURE 7

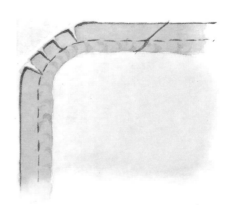

FIGURE 8

3. Cut the welting, leaving a 2″ tail, and stitch the welting to the section along the casing seam line. Remove the pins.

4. Place the welted section and the other section to be seamed with their right sides together. Stitch along the seam line as close to the welting as possible, leaving a 2″ gap for finishing.

finishing welting

1. Remove the stitches from the casing in the 2″ tail. Fold the casing back, exposing the extra 2″ of cord (Figure 9). Cut the cord so that it abuts the end of the other tail. Trim the extra casing so that ½″ extends beyond the cord (Figure 10).

2. Fold the extra ½″ of casing under ¼″ and lay it over the abutting end. Slipstitch the edges together (Figure 11).

3. Place the sections with the right sides together and stitch the gap closed on the seam line.

zippers

There are two kinds of zipper closures used in slipcovering. The placket zipper is sewn into the center of the slipcover back or across the back boxing of a cushion. The hidden zipper is sewn into a welted seam, and is virtually invisible. A zipper foot is highly recommended for either type. For large openings, use an industrial zipper with metal teeth. Refer to the individual projects for determining the length of the zipper you need.

placket zipper

1. Place the two sections to be joined right sides together and machine baste a ¾″ seam. Steam press the seam open.

2. With the wrong side of the fabric up, open the zipper and lay it fastener side down with the zipper teeth directly over the seam. Following the woven guideline on the zipper tape, hand baste the right side of the tape in place (Figure 1). Machine stitch directly over the basting stitches.

FIGURE 9
finishing welting

FIGURE 10

FIGURE 11

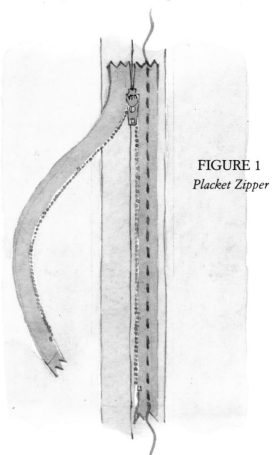

FIGURE 1
Placket Zipper

3. Close the zipper. Still working on the wrong side of the closure, baste the bottom ends and the remaining side of the zipper tape. Turn the fabric and zipper over, and working on the right side of the fabric, stitch over the basting along the bottom and the remaining side (Figure 2). Reinforce the top ends.

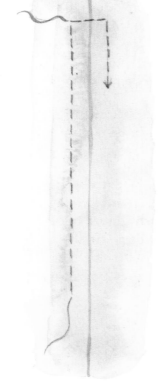

FIGURE 2

4. With small sharp-tipped scissors, snip the machine basting stitches that have kept the seam line closed during application of the zipper.

hidden zipper

1. Following the instructions for inserting welting, pages 140–141, stitch the welting to one of the two sections to be joined with a zipper.

2. Place the welted section right side up with the seam line to the right. Open the zipper and place it face down with the zipper teeth directly over the stitching line on the welting casing and pin (Figure 3).

3. Hand baste the zipper in place along the right side, close to the zipper teeth. Remove the pins, and machine stitch directly over the basting line. Fold over the zipper so its right side faces up.

4. On the unwelted section, press under a ¾″ seam allowance. Place the unwelted section right side up with the folded edge over the zipper tape and pin (Figure 4).

5. Hand baste ¼″ from the folded edge. Remove the pins, and machine stitch directly over the basting line. The ends of the zipper will be finished when the two sections are seamed.

Hidden Zipper

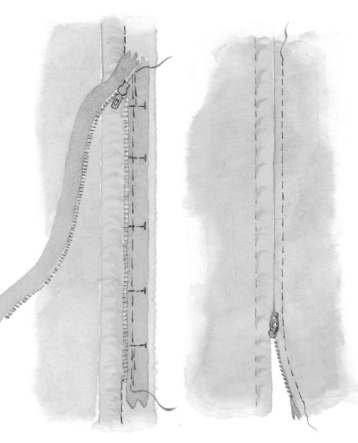

FIGURE 3   FIGURE 4

index

antique trims, 61
appliqué, 121–22
armchairs
    measuring, 64–66
    patterns for, 102–3
    sewing slipcovers for, 103–7
arm protectors, 119
arms
    fronts for, 76
    fronts for, 84
    measuring, 65
    patterns for, 81–82, 102
    sewing slipcovers for, 104–5

backstitching, 122
Baldwin, Billy, 10
bargain stores, 61
basting, 86, 122–23
bed linens, 57, 69
bias cutting, 94–95, 123
blanket stitching, 123
bolsters, 118–19
boudoir pillow shams, 90–93
box cushions, 103, 116–18
boxing, 85, 117
buttonholes, 123–24
buttons, 50, 51, 86, 123
buying fabrics, 56–61

cats, 76
chairs, 26–39
    measuring, 64–67
    patterns for, 79–85, 102–3
chaises, 20–23
    measuring, 64–66
    patterns for, 102–3
    sewing slipcovers for, 103–7
clipping, 124
closures, 86, 124
colors
    of fabrics, 54–55
    of trim, 49
cotton, 56
    bed linens of, 57
    steam pressing, 78
    testing, 58
cross stitching, 124
cushions
    box, 103, 116–18
    measuring, 66
cutting fabric, 101
    on bias, for pillow covers, 94–95
    patterns for, 78–85
    preparations for, 77
    railroading, 68

darts, 86, 125
daybeds, 20–25
    measuring, 67
    sewing slipcovers for, 110
decks, 106
de Wolfe, Elsie, 54–55
draped chair covers, 110
drapery panels, 58
drapery trims, 61
dressmaker's trims, 61
dry cleaning, 77

easing, 125
eyelets, 125–26

fabrics, 52–53, 126
    colors and patterns of, 54–55
    cutting, 101
    determining yardage needs for, 64
    preparation of, 77–78
    railroading (cutting), 68
    shopping for, 56–61
    weights of, 59–60
    widths of, 60
facing, 126
fibers, 56–57
fit of slipcovers, 11, 27, 119
flanged throws, 93

flannels, 57
fringes, 48–51, 51
furniture
    measuring, 64–68
    preparation of, 63

gathering, 127–28
grain, of fabric, 128
green, 54–55

hemstitches, 128

interfacing, 128
interior decorators, 60

layout strips, 68–75
linens, 57, 69
    steam pressing, 78
    testing, 58
linings, 59
    preparation of, 77
    skirt linings, 69
love seats, 10–17

machine washing, 77
measuring furniture, 64–68
medallion pillows, 98
motifs, centering, 101

natural fibers, 56–58

ottomans, 40–43
    measuring, 68
    sewing slipcovers for, 111

padding, 64
paisley, 55
passementerie, 48–51
patterns, for cutting, 78, 128
    cutting and pinning, 79–85
    marking, 101
patterns, of fabrics, 54–55, 69

pillows
    bias square cover for, 94–95
    boudoir shams for, 90–93
    covers for, 46–47, 88–89
    flanged throws for, 93
    ruffled round covers for, 96–97
    shirred medallion round covers
    for, 98
    turkish, 98–99
preparation
    of fabrics, 77–78
    of furniture, 63
    of pillow covers, 90
pre-shrinking fabrics, 77

quilting, 128–31

railroading, 68, 131
reinforcing, 131
repeating patterns, 69, 131
ruffled pillow covers, 96–97
ruffles, 132–33
running stitches, 132–32

scrimping, 69
seam allowances, 134
seam lines, 134
seams, 133
sections, 134
selvages, 134
sewing, 101
    basting, 86
    fabric weights selected for, 59–60
    patterns for, 78–85
    supplies for, 63
shams, 90–93
shirred medallion rounds, 98
shirring, 134–35
shopping for fabrics, 56–61
shoulders, of furniture, 85
    patterns for, 102
    sewing slipcovers for, 106
silk, 57

skirts, 69
    determining edges of, 79
    making, 112–15
slipper (armless) chairs, 38–39
    measuring, 66–67
    sewing slipcovers for, 108–9
slipstitching, 135
snap fasteners, 136
sofa beds, 107
sofas, 10–19
    measuring, 64–66
    patterns for, 79–85, 102–3
    sewing slipcovers for, 103–7
squaring edges, 77–78
staystitching, 136
steam pressing, 78, 136
supplies, sewing, 63
synthetic fabrics, 58

tassels, 48–51
ties, 136–37
topstitching, 137
trim finishing, 137–38
trimmings, 48–51, 61, 124
turkish pillows, 98–99

upholstery, fabrics for, 57

Velcro, 86, 139
vintage fabrics, 58

weights, of fabrics, 59–60
welting, 69, 101, 139–41
widths, of fabrics, 60
wings, of furniture
    patterns for, 85, 103
    sewing slipcovers for, 106
wool, 57

yardage of fabrics, 64, 76

zippers, 77, 86, 141–43